Jeff **Vines**

Dinner with
SKEPTICS

Defending God in a world that makes no sense

Dedication

To my wife Robin whose love sustains me.

To my daughter Sian
whose beauty mesmerizes me.

To my son Delaney who is my hero.

And to Milo who keeps sitting on the couch
when he is not supposed to.

Foreword

Some people analyze everything. Jeff Vines is definitely one of those people. I have often told him that he would be a much better golfer if he would stop thinking so much about "how" the golf club should be swung and "just swing it!" "Paralysis by analysis" is Jeff's nemesis on the golf course and, when playing a round where "loser buys lunch," I often take advantage of this weakness.

However, what stifles Jeff's golf game actually energizes the more important pursuits of his life. There are simply some issues that deserve a relentless pursuit toward understanding.

As a basketball coach I greatly empathize with Jeff in this regard. Watching hours of practice and game film and then successfully analyzing the defensive and offensive sets of our upcoming opponent can be the difference between winning and losing. No amount of effort is too great! And this is only a game!

For Jeff Vines, there is no greater pursuit than the pursuit of God. Understanding the way God works in this world and in our personal lives is paramount in Jeff's mind and deserves the greatest of analytical energies! And, his willingness to communicate his findings in such an "easy to read" style, makes this book a must for all who desire to give a clear and definitive reason for their hope and faith in God.

I truly wish I could have been with Jeff the night he had dinner with the skeptics in Brisbane, Australia. I can just see him as he asks question after question trying to assess why everyone is so angry with God, while, with humility, showing how such anger is unjustified.

As you will read, that night in Brisbane was filled with drama, passion, and suspense culminating in something far greater than a national championship in any sport. . . transformed lives!

Tony Bennett
Head Coach: Virginia Cavaliers
2007 NCAA Coach of the Year

Table of Contents

Introduction

*F*rom Zimbabwe, Africa, to Auckland, New Zealand, I have traveled around the world and heard some of the most fascinating stories. I once met a middle-aged woman in the bush of Africa who told me how she had been attacked by a crocodile while washing her family's clothes in the river. "The croc," she exclaimed, "snatched me from the water's edge, took me down to the river bed, and rolled me over and over trying to drown me!" Modestly she lifted the edge of her dress to reveal the impressive teeth marks beginning on her right shoulder and finishing just above the knee. She said, "But I outsmarted the old devil! I played like I was dead, and he went away to prepare himself for the feast.[1] While he was away, I climbed out of the river bed onto the shore and have never seen him since!"

Had I not seen the physical evidence, I would not have believed her story. How is it possible to survive such an attack? The thought of an African crocodile rolling a person (especially me) on the bottom of a river bed does not include a "what happens next" scenario. Once you're down, you're down. How is it possible to make a comeback?

Although for much of my adult life I have not lived in the United States, there is one thing about Americans I know for certain—Americans love comebacks! Whether in movies, sports, theater or in the everyday workplace, we love it when someone seems down for the count only to make an awe-inspiring recovery. In fact, one of my favorite lines from a sports commentator came from CBS golf analyst Verne Lundquist. Jack Nicklaus, perhaps the greatest golfer of all time, entered the 1986 Masters Tournament at a time when the sun seemed to be setting on his illustrious career. But someone forgot to tell Nicklaus he was too old to win. Jack made a final round charge, shot 29 on the back nine at Augusta National, and won the most coveted prize in golf at the ripe old age of 46. When Nicklaus drained an eagle putt on the fifteenth green on the way to his victory, Lundquist exclaimed, "The Bear [Nicklaus's nickname] has come out of hibernation!" America applauded, golfers and nongolfers were inspired, and one of the greatest comebacks of all time was recorded in the history books.

Unfortunately, sometimes the recovery for which we so desperately long does not come. A parent loses a child. A child loses a parent. A disease remains uncured. A habit remains unbroken. Every trip around the sun brings the hope of recovery, but sometimes recovery just doesn't come. Instead, greater loss occurs and the effects are tragic.

This book is about recovering something that is lost. Something we lost that unless recovered yields perhaps the worst possible ramifications known to the human experience. Such loss inevitably leads to meaninglessness and depression, dejection and hopelessness, despondency and despair. In fact, unless that which is lost is recovered, nothing that is found matters. A life of joy, peace, and prosperity will remain elusive, and any sort of satisfaction will be temporary at best.

Indeed, can God make a comeback? Although God has never moved, our accusations against Him have convinced many that He has ridden off into the sunset never to return. Even those who acknowledge his existence expect very little from Him and live pragmatically as atheists. "God may exist," they say, "but His existence makes little difference to my life."

This book is about a woman who believed that God's recovery was about as likely as a tornado sweeping through a junkyard and assembling a fully functioning Boeing 747.[2] Harmonizing what we know about this world with the existence of God, in her mind, was just not possible. God was just too far gone. He could not recover.

My desire is that through the words on these pages, I can transport you back to the events that led to Laura's rediscovering or recovering God. Her story has as much tension and intrigue as any novel I have read. These events are actual and occurred, not in the jungle of Africa nor the mountains of New Zealand, but in a place least expected. After all. the most fascinating and inspiring stories do not happen in the unfamiliar far off places of the world, but in the concrete jungles with which we are all too familiar.

Chapter One

Life's Most Intriguing Question

*A*s I glanced up from a great cup of coffee in the hotel café, I noticed an attractive young woman quickly approaching. She walked with intent, stopped at my table, and introduced herself, "My name is Laura, and I am the hotel manager," and proceeded to recite what sounded like a speech from the local tourism board. She was the consummate professional, with every hair in place and each stroke of the makeup brush carefully applied. She completed her introduction to the hotel and began to walk away. Although impressed, I lowered my head back toward the newspaper and continued to enjoy my café latté—the moment's top priority!

The click clack of expensive high heels as she made her way back to my table interrupted my latté festivity. "What do you do, Mr. Vines?" Laura asked. At first, I thought, *are you serious?* Up until that point her conversation had been, although extremely articulate, mostly impersonal. Giving her the benefit of the doubt, I informed her of my profession and waited for a response. I was surprised when I saw the sudden smirk on her face. With no verbal response she did an about face and simply walked away. I thought, "Wow! What was that all about?" Minutes passed, and again, those little high heels marched toward me for a third time. As my latté rapidly cooled, Laura said, "Mr. Vines, I would like to extend an invitation to you to join my staff and me for dinner tonight. Would you kindly accept my invitation?" I am not sure what shocked me the most: Laura's invitation to a free meal, or the manner in which she invited me. I learned later that Laura ran such a tight ship that she dined with her staff each evening in order to keep a close eye over all the activities and to discuss the day's successes and failures while giving the imperious orders to the coming shift.

Moreover, I was later informed that no outsider had ever been invited to this 'knights of the round table' discussion group, and the fact that I had been issued such an invitation was nothing short of a miracle!

Perhaps I should have been more concerned about her motivations, but the possibility of a fine dining experience overshadowed any concern I might have had about her intentions. After all, having looked deeply into many of life's questions, I have come to understand some answers will always elude us. However, one area is extremely clear to me. It concerns the question, "What is life really about?" My conclusion? And I think you will agree—free food! So, I accepted the invitation.

6 P.M. The night at the round table begins . . .

When I arrived at the banquet, my suspicions intensified. A designated place at the end of a long table with my name engraved on a flowery card pointed clearly to my place in the arena. Laura took her seat at the opposite end, made the necessary introductions, and smugly glanced in my direction. With everyone looking intently my way, I took one sip of Diet Coke, breathed deeply, and waited for the trouble to begin. I was certain that something unpleasant was brewing.

Only seconds passed before Dan, a police officer employed by the hotel as a part-time security director, broke the silence. As soon as he spoke, I got the feeling he had drawn the short straw and had been designated as the one who would 'get the ball rolling.' After taking a big gulp of his Australian beer, he slammed his glass down on the table, winked at his peers, then turned toward me and dropped the bomb!

"So, Jeff, how can you believe in God with all the evil in this world!? Have you ever heard of the Holocaust? Stalin? Lenin? War? Starving children? Tsunamis? Earthquakes? Wake up, man! There is no God!"

Stunned, I thought, *Wow, so this is what this is all about.* While Laura seemed proud of the manner in which Dan had delivered his philosophical dart, the look on Dan's face and his Barney Fife-type grin exposed his pride and revealed his lack of expectation for any kind of logical response. In his eyes, this was a fail-proof accusation. No comeback was possible. His statement (although formed as a question) was the end of the matter—so, let's eat! Laura, on the other hand, apparently craved a night of entertainment in the form of God-bashing. At the time I did not know their reasons or motivations for wanting to do away with God. One thing was certain: in Dan's mind the conversation was over. Nothing more needed to be said.

I reviewed Dan's assumption as I took another sip of Diet Coke. According to Dan, war, death, and the devastation of people and this planet could not possibly be harmonized with the existence of a "higher being." The two could not possibly coexist. His statement seemed incredibly similar to the words of David Hume, an infamous eighteenth-century skeptic who complained:

> Were a stranger to drop suddenly into this world, I would show him as a specimen of its ills a hospital full of diseases,

a prison crowded with malefactors and debtors, a field strewn with carcasses, a fleet floundering in the ocean, a nation languishing under tyranny, famine or pestilence. Honestly, I don't see how you can possibly square with the ultimate purpose of love.[3]

Similarly, from Dan's perspective, he had made his statement, no defense was possible, and that was the end of that!

Where Is God?

I cleared my throat, gathered my thoughts, and looked toward Dan to ask him a question he was not expecting: "Dan, can you and I interact on this issue for a moment?"

"What do you mean?" he responded.

"Well, you have asked a great question, but I think the question itself needs to be analyzed. Would you help me with this issue?"

Hesitantly, but confidently, Dan said, "Sure. What do you want?"

"Well, first of all, once you admit that there is such a thing as 'evil' in the world, are you not also assuming that there is such a thing as 'good'?[4] After all, how can anyone know the definition of 'evil' unless he knows the definition of 'good'?"

Puzzled, Dan took another sip of beer and responded, "If you are asking me if I know how to tell the difference between 'good' and 'evil,' then my answer is, 'Yes, I think we all can.'"

I agreed and continued, "So then, if we admit 'good' as a category and 'evil' as a separate and distinct category, how do we know what event goes into which category? Who or what tells us what is 'evil' and what is 'good'?"

Dan's response was both quick and typical, "Jeff," he replied, "I already said that it is not rocket science! We all know the difference between 'good' and 'evil.'"

Time Out!

Now before we continue let us make sure we understand Dan's presupposition. He is implying that the ability to distinguish between 'good' and 'evil' is universal and that such ability is innate.

Dan claimed we all have a sense of right and wrong. Although Dan did not use the words 'moral law,' one would be hard pressed to deny that this is exactly what he meant: that inside all of us is a moral law which enables us to distinguish between 'right' and 'wrong' and grants us the ability to categorize both the corporate and the individual's actions as either 'good' or 'evil.'

Back to the Story

I seized the opportunity and rebutted, "But, Dan, if there is a 'moral law' somewhere that tells us what events, actions, or reactions should be filed under the category of 'evil' and what events, actions, or reactions should be filed under the category of 'good,' then would that moral law not have to be 'absolute' or unchanging?"

"What do you mean?" Dan quickly parried.

"Well, for evil to be evil, it must be evil in all times, places, and circumstances," I said. "Otherwise, God could give a defense to your accusation by saying, 'Dan, you accuse Me of allowing evil in the world, but the reality is that if you just wait long enough, what you see as evil will one day become good.'"

"Are you saying that there is no such thing as good and evil?" Dan angrily replied.

"No," I said, "I agree that there are categories of 'good' and 'evil' and that men and women everywhere have a basic understanding of these categories; but I want you to understand that, unless these categories are absolute, then any accusation made against anyone becomes indefensible."

Hitler's Rationale

A crucial argument in a postmodern world rejects absolute morality and then attempts to invoke an absolute moral law on the Hitlers, Stalins, and Lenins of the world. You should have seen the look on Dan's face as I described the following scenario.

"Suppose we could board a time machine, travel back into Nazi Germany where we could obtain permission to hold a one-on-one interview with Adolph Hitler. As we sit in the chair adjacent to his Evilness, suppose we say, 'Hitler, you are an evil man! You took the lives of innocent men, women, and children. You wreaked havoc upon humanity and committed all kinds of atrocities against the human race. You murdered over six million Jews and are responsible for the deaths of many others. You are a bad man! Internally, I have placed your deeds into the category of evil! Shame on you!'

"Now, what if Hitler responds (and there is a good chance he would say precisely this) by saying, 'I beg to differ. In fact, as I see it, I am a 'good' man who tried to rid my country of a race of people who had tarnished and poisoned humanity with its corrupted blood line. I employed the "final solution" in an attempt to purify and protect my people and advance the evolutionary cycle toward perfection and the survival of the fittest. How can you say that I am evil? I am highly offended by your accusation and acknowledge that your limited understanding of the universe has narrowed your thinking.'"

"What is your point?" Dan asked, confused.

"Clearly," I said, "unless there is an absolute moral law somewhere that classifies as 'evil,' murdering children in gas ovens, shooting entire families at point blank range, and exterminating an entire people group through starvation and torture, then Hitler would have a point to make, would he not?"

I continued, "Do you see the irony of the university professor who claims that morality is situational, that 'right' and 'wrong' are left up to the individual, and then states categorically that Hitler was wrong to commit his horrendous acts upon humanity? An absolute accusation requires an absolute moral law to which everyone must conform."

This was the argument given by an American lawyer at the Nuremburg trials. The generals of the Third Reich who assisted Hitler in carrying out the "final solution," said they were only obeying the law of their land and therefore could not be held responsible for their actions. After hours and hours of their ridiculous defense, the American lawyer finally threw his hands up in frustration and asked, "Is there not a law above our laws? Is there not an authority higher than our authority to which all men, regardless of the mandate of any political leader, must be held accountable?"

Self-Evident Truths

The origin of the moral law within every human heart is perhaps one of the greatest objective proofs of God's existence. No matter where you travel in this world, absolute moral law exists within every culture. Equally astounding is the fact that even in communist, war-torn countries where God has been thrown out of the public arena, the masses continue to live in testimony to His existence in private. In fact, people in communist countries possess a moral law that is astonishingly similar to those nations in which religion is not restricted, where God is alive and well. Well-known apologist Ravi Zacharias, in his book, *Cries of the Heart*, illustrates a strikingly consistent moral law that both transcends culture and is written deep within the human heart.

> It (the play) was a story of a young peasant who married a lovely young village woman. As they were blissfully on their journey to another village to set up their own home, the prince of the land traveling with his soldiers was captured by her beauty and demanded that the peasant give

her to him as a palace concubine. The peasant resisted valiantly, and so by force, the prince grabbed the woman and took her away with him.

Dismayed and heartsick, the peasant hastened to the palace to beg the king to intercede for him and to return his wife. The king was outraged by the poor man's charge and contended that the woman came by her own volition to live with the prince. To prove his point the king ordered the woman to be brought to the palace hearing. When she was led before him, he demanded that she acknowledge who her real husband was. The moment of truth came and all were gathered in the palace hall to hear her words.

Behind the scenes, of course, the king had threatened the woman that if she admitted that the peasant was indeed her husband, he would be taken away and killed. The woman therefore, in great fear, when challenged by the authority in court softly but with evident trepidation pointed to the prince as her actual husband. The court went into uproar, cheering the king, and the peasant cowered under the weight of his rejection.

The priest watching these proceedings demanded an inquiry and then announced to the people that something seemed wrong with the whole scenario. "Why would an ordinary man risk the rage of the king by claiming that the prince's wife was his? I have the perfect solution to get the truth," he said. He then proceeded to lay out a simple plan based on what he claimed was a foolproof truth serum. "I will give both the prince and the peasant an equal dose of the serum, and within ten minutes the effect will take place. Knowing that one of them is telling a lie and will be punished by death for the crime, I suggest that each of these men be given five minutes alone with the woman, with no physical contact between them."

A huge barrel suspended from the midpoint of a pole held horizontally was brought to the stage. It was so large that it took two people, one shouldering each end of the pole, to carry this unwieldy equipment. The instructions were given. The woman was to carry one end of the pole while each of the men in turn was to carry the other end, separated by the barrel. They could walk away to a secluded setting prior to returning for the verdict. Each had five minutes with the woman.

During the time she had with the prince, he did nothing but harangue her and threaten her with her husband's death if she ever spoke the truth.

When the time came for her to be alone with her husband, it was fascinating to watch even the subtle hints of his love for her. He did his best to position himself so that he would carry the brunt of weight of the barrel and protect her from any strain. During the time they were alone she wept and spoke of her undying love for him and explained that the only reason she had lied was to spare his life. "If they had threatened my life, I could take it, but I could not bear to see you die," she said. He understood her plight and said that he would only speak the truth.

They returned to a suspense-filled courtroom, and, I might add, to an audience filled even more with anticipation, all of us sitting at the edge of our seats. As all was readied for the serum to take effect, the priest announced that the truth would now triumph over the lie.

At that moment the barrel burst open and out jumped a little boy who had been hiding inside. He carried a pen and a pad in his hand and had copied down all he had heard during the private conversations the men had when each was alone with the woman. The young boy turned over his notes to the priest. The priest read what they contained, and as he watched the prince lower his head and the peasant's face shine with the radiance of returned love, he declared the truth. The audience in the auditorium could not contain its jubilation and roared with approval, only to see tragedy strike as the king ordered his soldiers to kill all who believed the young boy's version of the conversations.

"Anyone in Cambodia knew the double-edged tragedy of the play." Ravi continues, "The voice of truth had been silenced, and cruel men ruled the land, inflicting fear on the people." As Ravi remained seated in contemplation long after the conclusion of the theatrical production, he tells how he began to reflect on "how behind the drama lies some common values that bind humanity: the purity of marital love; the value of truth; the cry to protect the innocent; the wickedness of unbridled power and the undying yearning of a people to see justice roll on like a river."[5]

In one line of summation, Zacharias delivers a powerful thought when he concludes: "These were not conferred culturally. The truths were self-evident even in a Marxist-dominated land."[6]

Time Out!

Though we protest absolute moral law, we invoke it when we feel as though we are on the receiving end of injustice. I once debated a professor in Hawaii who prided himself on denying absolute moral law of any kind until I asked him to give me a situation where it could be considered "right" for someone to invade his home at night, kidnap his little granddaughter, rape, and torture her until death. As his granddaughter waited intently for his answer, he found it hard to offer a situation for such an ethic.

Back to the Story

After hearing that 'good' and 'evil' as absolute categories can only exist if an absolute moral law is present to sustain them, I asked Dan if he knew anyone who had the knowledge and authority to give this absolute moral law to which all humanity must conform.

"Well, it's sure not the religious hypocrites of this world or people like you!" Dan responded in anger.

In wholehearted agreement, I confirmed that all men were tainted by their finiteness and could not possibly give an absolute moral law under which the rest of humanity should live. Such absolute law could only originate from an absolute moral lawgiver. Only the creator and sustainer of all things would have the authority, knowledge, and power to implant within all creatures the ability to distinguish between 'good' and 'evil.'

What is most interesting is the fact that no matter where you go in the world, the basic understanding of right and wrong exists, and only when evil men set out to tarnish and corrode such understanding do the atrocities of our world occur. Creating a 'killing' culture as Hitler successfully achieved required years of propaganda, brainwashing, and, in fact, an unlearning of the basics of right and wrong. Rome was not built in a day; neither was Germany. You and I look at the horrific acts associated with Hitler's "final solution" with great disdain and judgment. Indeed we should. But we should remember that before Hitler could build his edifices, the old foundations of absolute moral law had to be destroyed. With the absence of absolute moral law, Hitler created a killing machine.

Reminding Dan of this lesson from history, I moved toward a summary of my response.

"Dan," I exclaimed, "without an absolute moral law which defines the absolute categories of 'good' and 'evil,' the world would not be able to stand up and shout, 'Stop! This is wrong! This is unjust! This is evil!' Without this absolute moral law we would have no foundation on which to stand when screaming out against the atrocities and injustices of our world. You have admitted that such categories exist, but in the next breath deny the existence of the only One who can give this absolute moral law. Dan," I said, with a kind and gentle voice, "without God there is no such thing as 'evil,' for only the One who has created all things holds the right to give the rules by which creation should be governed. Yet God is the one you are trying to disprove. This faulty logic is similar to using a butterfly to disprove the existence of a caterpillar. One cannot exist without the other."

Looking for an Exit!

At this point, Dan wished he had never been born, or at least had never come to this dinner. Fidgeting and noticeably disturbed, Laura sat at the other end of the table with a look of deep concern. The entertainment (me) had not fulfilled her hopes and ambitions. While every staff member around the table sat in frustration, Dan asked a question that could not have been scripted more perfectly. His query served as the most logical next step in our journey toward God. He demanded, "OK, Jeff, then you tell me what kind of God allows so much evil into His world?"

Wow, I thought, *in a matter of minutes Dan had made the journey from "There is absolutely no God!" to "Perhaps God exists but He is not kind!"*

In a much softer voice, I placed my hand on Dan's shoulder and responded, "Dan, I think, down deep inside, the real issue you are struggling with is not God's existence, but the manner in which He governs His creation. In short, you are trying to harmonize the existence of God with all the evil, pain, and suffering in our world. Your first assumption that 'God' and 'evil' cannot coexist lacks sufficient understanding of both God and evil. Without God, there is no need to ask the question of evil. In fact, there is no reason to ask any question. The 'why' question can only be asked when God is assumed."

Evolution's premise, that we are simply a collection of chemicals bouncing to-and-fro reminds us that nature is red in tooth and claw and you and I are at the mercy of natural selection. Make no mistake, as soon as you assume evil, you assume God. As soon as you ask, "Why?" you imply purpose and meaning in the universe. Such valuable commodities cannot exist without a higher cause.

Dan's failure to debunk God led to a long moment of silence and deep contemplation. It soon became clear, however, that Dan's failure meant that others must now attempt an offensive of their own. In no way had I intended to embarrass him but his pride got the better of him, and he began to drown his sorrow in his glass of beer. Dan, in fact, would end up being my only regret of the evening. His opening remarks and the ensuing conversation sparked a change in everyone around that table, except for perhaps himself. For Dan, it was not a battle for corporate truth, but a far less important battle for intellectual bragging rights. If only he had not spent the rest of the evening sulking, he might have had the life changing encounter we all were about to experience.

A Quick Application

The questions we ask about life, meaning, purpose, and even the predicament of the universe, presume so much. The next time you are having a moment of deep reflection that sparks a troubling question, stop and think for a moment about the question itself. Our questions are often built upon primary assumptions. For instance, the question, "Why am I experiencing this tragedy in my life?" is built upon two inescapable assumptions.

Assumption one is that a reason for your suffering exists; that your pain is not the result of merely bad luck. Somehow, somewhere, in the deepest regions of the universe, reason and purpose do indeed exist for the trials of your life.

Assumption two is that the reasons for your pain are discoverable; that you are capable of seeing beyond the temporary pain into eternal purposes and plans which bring ultimate meaning to every experience of your life, good or bad. The questions we ask about pain are seldom rhetorical. We ask questions because we desperately seek meaningful and coherent answers.

The point is that both of the assumptions listed above go a long way toward helping us find the answers. For instance, finding purpose to the tragedies of our lives is possible only when there is meaning and purpose to this universe in the first place! This is something that an accidental, blind, dumb-luck planet cannot give you. In reality, if there is no God, there is no reason, purpose, or meaning to anything.

Ah! But when God exists, as our intuitive questions and assumptions often verify, we can find the answers to life's most penetrating questions. After all, will the One who placed these assumptions within us not also help us discover the answers? Otherwise, why lodge the questions deep into our consciences?

When all is said and done, I think you will find that part of the Creator's way of communicating His existence to us is by placing an internal desire and need to find an answer to the "whys" of our lives—answers which can only be found in a world that has arrived by intention. For the God who allows tragedy into our lives is the same God who desperately desires to explain the origin and purpose for suffering and the way to live above and beyond our pain.

Chapter Two

The Highest Value in the Universe

*L*aura and her staff looked noticeably uncomfortable as they waited for someone to rescue Dan out
of this pit of despair. Sherri, seated on my left side, directly
across the table from Dan, waited to unleash her own assault. A
philosophy major at a local university, she was chomping at the
bit to get her hooks into me. I could feel the hair standing on the
back of my neck as she waited patiently for the dialogue between
Dan and me to end. At her first opportunity, Sherri complained,
"OK, Jeff, I know what you are doing here! I have studied much
philosophy and know how you self-proclaimed theologians work!
You are professionals at playing with words!"

7:15 P.M. Asking the big question . . .

I must confess I was quite taken aback by Sherri's
accusation. After all, this was the precise manner in which I
would describe every philosopher I had ever met—'players with

words.' They seem more than willing to climb higher and higher up the ladder of abstraction without coming to any real conclusions about anything, except of course that there are no real conclusions.

At the risk of insulting Sherri and nullifying any chance I had to continue this conversation, I decided to try to convince her that a greater issue was at stake. Gently ignoring her remark and moving ahead in the conversation, I asked her to explain the weakness in my argument thus far. She interrupted immediately and said, "No, I will not answer your questions; I would like you to answer mine! Jeff, you keep putting us on the back foot with your questions! Why don't you answer ours for a change?"

Obviously, Sherri was upset. Any time the "God" issue surfaces, emotions surge and tempers fly, most often to the point of irrationality. How can it be that something so important cannot be discussed in a peaceful, logical, productive fashion amongst rational human beings? In fact, I am all too well aware that many who begin to read this book will stop as soon as the word "God" is mentioned. Why is this? Most often, I find the answer involves one of two issues: unfulfilled expectations or hypocritical converts. Concerning unfulfilled expectations: anger toward God due to the feeling that life has not been fair is not uncommon. When God does not do what we think He ought to do, we often become like little children in a candy store screaming, "I hate you," at our parents because they won't buy us what we believe to be rightfully ours. Concerning hypocritical converts: a favorite author of mine emphatically states that the problem with faith in God is not a lack of evidence but a failure on the part of those who believe to live it out.[7] No doubt, unfulfilled dreams and hypocritical people are perhaps two of the greatest enemies to belief in God.

Nevertheless, even in a secular country like New Zealand where there is an aggressive campaign by the liberal media to expel God from the culture, God still gets major media coverage. Not a day goes by when the national radio station or the national newspaper does not bring up the "God" question. For ten years I stood before over ten thousand New Zealanders each weekend and reminded them that for a country that does not believe God exists, He sure gets a lot of press.

Considering this, I cautiously addressed her by gently asking, "What is your question?" Sherri belted back with, "If God is so good, gracious, and kind, then why is there so much pain in this world? Have you seen the pictures of those starving children? Where is the loving God that the Christians talk so much about?"

Time Out!

I must point out that although there are certain similarities between Dan's and Sherri's questions, a world of difference still exists. While Dan attempted to employ the presence of evil as a tool to deny the very existence of God; Sherri's endeavor seemed to assume God's existence but questioned the very nature and character of this absolute being. In other words, Sherri was not denying that God exists but was questioning whether or not Christians, or any other religion, had correctly understood His nature. What is God really like? Is He actually a God of love and power? Or, is He a God of apathy and impotence? Moreover, if God exists, why on earth did He originate a creation scenario where little children suffer from hunger, abuse, and ultimately, death? Remember Dan's accusation—"Have you ever heard of the Holocaust? Stalin? Lenin? War? Starving children? Tsunamis? Earthquakes?—Wake up, man! There is no God!"

Honest Questions

If religious people are honest, these questions may be demanding, but they are also fair! Only those whose faith is shallow or blind would ignore or belittle such questions. Sherri asked a legitimate question that deserved contemplation and explanation before proceeding.

My conversation with Dan had taken over an hour. While the mood around the table was still hostile, something interesting began to occur. Although most around the table assumed that the night's intriguing conversation was about to come to an end, every eye reflected a ray of hope that perhaps some solution could solve their dilemmas and restore hope to the brokenhearted. In fact, I am convinced that Sherri was merely verbalizing the pain and turmoil in the lives of everyone around that table. There is a part of all of us that wants to believe in a Creator. Without such faith, rational beings know that there is no real hope, meaning, or purpose to the lives we live and the heartache we endure. The presence of enormous pain and suffering in our world does make it extremely difficult to embrace the idea of a God of love and kindness.

Life's Great Irony

I have always found it ironic that the New Zealand education system insists upon aggressively indoctrinating its citizens that a belief in God is only for those whose minds are limited, whose internal fortitude is weak, and whose grasp on reality is null and void. Yet, as soon as someone experiences the loss of a close relative or attends the funeral of a grandma or grandpa, uncle or auntie, all of a sudden, people talk about a "better place" to which we all go after death. Everyone stands around after the service, drinking a cup of tea, talking about the "goodness" of the deceased, and how s/he is now in the midst of peace and tranquility. The word "heaven" may not be used, but the adjectives used to describe this "better place" are identical to the age-old words and phrases used to describe heaven. A place called "heaven" that offers peace, rest, and a life beyond compare has not lost its popularity even in a secular, atheistic country. But where is the logic in this? Heaven without God? Surely this is intellectual bankruptcy. *How could there be a heaven without a God who cares enough to create such a place?* Surely we are not suggesting that the "big bang" exploded heaven into existence? The truth is, in the same way that "evil" as an absolute category cannot exist without God so, also, heaven is contingent upon the good intentions of the Absolute.

Table Manners

Nevertheless, Sherri's question was on the table, "How can people claim that God is good, loving, and kind with all the pain and suffering we see in our world?" With everyone in the room leaning forward, waiting for my reply, I felt somewhat frustrated by the fact that, although I had a rational, logical answer to give, I was afraid someone around the table may not be asking the question in the abstract but in the personal sense. Giving a philosophically sound answer to someone who presently was enduring a difficult situation (the loss of a loved one, the death of a child, the breakup of a relationship) might seem cold and heartless. Therefore, looking intently in the eyes of each questioner, I again proceeded with caution and attempted to bathe my response in love.

Truth Is Closer Than We Think

Ironically, right before our eyes was the perfect illustration that would sustain the truth. Seated next to Sherri was her boyfriend Richard. Most guys will understand what I mean when I say that Richard liked Sherri a lot more that Sherri liked Richard. For the entire evening, Richard could not keep his hands off Sherri! Infatuated, if not mesmerized by this young lady (she was indeed attractive), Richard refused to accept the fact that she did not return his affections. Working with Sherri day in and day out must have been a thrill for him. To wake up each day and know that the woman of your dreams will be in close proximity for the next eight hours seemed, I am sure, like a dream to Richard. Sure, Sherri may have thought he was cute—she did invite him to sit beside her and to share the evening meal, but this relationship was undeniably one-sided. The fact that everyone knew this made Richard the perfect candidate for a bit of role playing. So, respectfully, and with Laura keeping a close eye on things, "Richard," I asked, "Do you mind if I use you as an example as I attempt to answer Sherri's question?"

"Me? You want me as an example?" he responded.

Remember, he saw what happened to Dan so, naturally, was cautious. Yet, he faced a dilemma. On the one hand, this may be his chance to impress Sherri and come to her defense as a knight in shining armor. On the other hand, a situation where he might be embarrassed might widen the distance between them. The tension was undeniably visible. Yet in the end, chivalry won the battle and Richard reluctantly, but assuredly, agreed to play the part.

"Richard," I said, "what if I told you that I could give you a microchip that you could implant in Sherri's brain? Accompanying this gadget is a miniature computer that would enable you to program Sherri to do, think, and say everything you wanted her to do, think, and say? Would you like that?"

The mere thought of such a contraption sent Richard into a momentary fantasy world. Although he attempted to hide his dream, we all knew what he was thinking. Even more intriguing was the fact that every male at the table, hoping to obtain an edge over the opposite sex, simultaneously leaned forward as if involved in a synchronized swimming event. They were waiting for the unveiling of this secret device. (Witnessing all this firsthand, I began to think that perhaps my wife is right when she says, "Men are the shallowest of all creatures.")

Richard, thinking that he could preprogram Sherri to say things like, "Richard, you are the most handsome man on the planet." "Richard, what would you like me to make you for dinner?" "Richard, I will love you and only you for the rest of my life," moved him in such a dramatic fashion that he stumbled over his words as he blurted out, "Yeees! Ab—b-bb solutely! Where can I get it?" Upon hearing his response, Sherri gave Richard a look with which every husband is extremely familiar.

For a moment I believe Richard actually thought I had this contraption and was about to open my coat and offer him a special discount! With every male anticipating and every female thoroughly disgusted, I responded to Richard's confidence by demanding, "No, you would not!"

"What do you mean?" he said.

"Richard, the truth is that down deep inside this is not what you really want. You would not want to possess such an invention," I replied.

"Sure I would," he responded.

Shaking my head, I urged him to consider what all this really meant. "How long," I asked "would it be until Sherri would mean nothing to you?"

Confused, he exclaimed, "What do you mean?"

"Richard," I replied, "after a while, nothing Sherri said or did would be meaningful since nothing stated or spoken originated from a personal, free, decision. You are not alone in wanting to be honored, respected, and ultimately, loved by someone. However, the irony is that for love to be genuine and authentic, it must be given freely. Love can be compelled and encouraged but it cannot be forced or demanded. In other words, true love between two people can only exist if both have the freedom to give, receive, or reject that love."

I am convinced that this is not philosophical mumbo jumbo. This is about as real as life gets. Love can only be love when it is given freely. We can force someone to be a slave. We can force someone to enter into all kinds of illicit acts. But we can never force someone to love us. This is something that every man who has attempted to win the heart of a woman understands.

The Courting Metaphor

As a youngster my dream, along with millions of other American boys, was to play baseball in the big leagues. The fact that I did not have the talent essential to the task did not deter me. Everything took a back seat to baseball practice. In fact, strangely enough, my interest in the opposite sex did not really kick in until I went away to university. Don't misunderstand, the young girls of East Tennessee where I grew up definitely caught my eye, but the time required to have a girlfriend seemed such a waste. All the talking on the telephone, the parties, and mall wandering seemed a distraction from my ultimate goal. Looking back, I now know that the real problem was that I simply had not met the right girl. Only a few days after enrolling as a freshman in college, just a couple of days passed until I met the most beautiful woman I had ever seen. She had lily-white skin, deep blue eyes, and curves in all the right places. She sent me into a lasting daze. Indeed, I was mesmerized! Suddenly, nothing else mattered. I now had but one purpose—to win the heart of this elegant, sleek, and captivating woman.

Realizing the odds were heavily against me, I began to put a plan of coercion and manipulation into action. I know those are harsh words, but in reality this is exactly what every man does. Who he is before marriage and who he is after is an unparalleled contrast. Before I was married, I could do heroic things. I could carry five pieces of luggage through the airport without looking remotely stretched or undone. I could jump out of a car on a rainy night, sprint around to the other side, hold an umbrella over a young woman's head, and escort her into a building. All of this without one drop of water coming anywhere near her beautiful, perfectly formed body. I could make rose petals appear day after day as if I owned all the roses in the world and could dispense them at will, unlimited by time and space. After marriage, however, things changed. In the airport, I would pick up two pieces of luggage and complain, "Are you coming or not?" On a rainy night I began to sit and wait for my new wife to get out of the car and open the garage door so that my unattractive, quickly deteriorating body could remain dry. And finally, my ability to produce roses quickly faded. In fact, I am not even sure what they look like anymore. Are roses those reddish-type flowers?

Anyway, Superman lives at least until the wedding when the kryptonite of self-centeredness kicks in. The point is: no computer chip exists, and every man knows this. He knows he must woo the woman he loves. He must court her. He must draw her unto himself by showering her with gifts of love and affection, hoping that one day she will notice his efforts, trust his motives, and give her heart to him willingly. Although it's hard and we men often complain, if we really thought about it, we really would not want it any other way. After all, *when we men win the heart of a woman, it's not only the fact that she has given her heart to us, but that she has given her heart to us instead of our competitors*. If this was a book about marriage, we would include an entire chapter concerning what Bill Hybels calls the "pursuing" and "treasuring" of our wife long after the marriage ceremony has ended.[8] This wooing and treasuring during the courting phase is supposed to continue throughout the marriage. There would be far fewer broken relationships in this world and far more satisfied and fulfilled men and women if such wooing and treasuring continued. However, we will leave such discussions for the relationship books.

Surely, love is our greatest pursuit, most intense emotion, and undoubtedly the highest value of our universe. Why else would we risk so much pain for the hope of so much pleasure? Nazareth performed an interesting song about love, a song that repeatedly proclaims the thoughts of the masses: Love hurts, love scars, love wounds and mars, love hurts! Ooo-oo Love hurts![9]

True, love risks great despair. Yet the risk of such despondency never stops us from seeking the unrealized. We may feel like Nazareth, but rest assured, when the opportunity for love approaches, although cautious, we still take the plunge! Why? Every human heart knows that the reward of finding genuine, authentic, true love is worth risking everything.

From Ooo to Woo

Having expressed these ideas in a humorous and light-hearted fashion, Laura and her friends began to lighten up a bit and embrace me as an "OK guy" who perhaps had at least half a brain.

Sensing the mood, I moved forward, continuing to build the foundation upon which I would fashion together an apology that would seek to harmonize a loving God with a universe that featured pain and suffering.

So, jovially, I asked Sherri if she had seen the movie *Bruce Almighty*. If you are familiar with the movie you will recall that Jim Carey plays the role of a man whose life is falling apart. As a result, Bruce continually complains that "God could fix my life in five minutes if He really wanted to." God hears his cry and decides to endow Bruce with all His powers. Instead of helping others with his special gifts, Bruce selfishly helps himself. Moreover, failing to remember God's *quid pro quo* (God does not mess with free will, neither can Bruce), Bruce attempts to force his girlfriend to love him. He leaps onto a ledge and tries to call upon his powers to force her affection. Rendering a contorted expression and stretching arms wide open, attempting to harness all the power of the Almighty, Bruce demands, "Love me! Love me! Love me!" Yet, to no avail. Love must be given freely.

Weary of all of this Sherri interrupted and asked, "Enough, Jeff, what does love and free will have to do with all the pain and suffering in the world? We asked you about pain, and all you've been talking about is love and freedom! What do these things have to do with my question?"

"Absolutely everything!" I responded. "Once God decided that love would be the hallmark of His creation, a great tension must have arisen. On the one hand, He desires intimacy, love, and relationship with those whom He creates. He desires to shower His goodness upon all humanity and to grant such gifts as sunshine, rain, oceans, mountains, rivers, and streams. He grants a vivid reminder each new evening as the sun sets and the stars shine of His awesome ability to create and sustain a universe so expansive that even the brightest, sharpest minds cannot comprehend its fine tuning and intricate design. But why does He do it? Why does He provide such awesome scenes? Is this God's way of wooing us to Himself without violating free will?"

The Ultimate Wooing!

Sherri interrupted again, "Yes, Jeff, I see your point, but what does this have to do with pain and suffering in this world?" I asked Sherri if she could bear with me for one more quick illustration before moving directly to the issue. She responded, "Yes, if you promise to get to the point." I agreed and continued,

"Sherri, after I wooed my wife into marriage, she wooed me to Africa! She constantly told me of the beautiful sights and wonderful people and culture. By the time I graduated university, I was primed and ready to move to Zimbabwe, Africa, and start a new life with my new wife. I must confess that the saying, 'Africa gets into your blood,' is categorically true. From the animals to the plains, to the stars in the sky and the red setting sun, Zimbabwe introduced me to a world I never knew existed. New Zealand, with all its wonderful sights, can never surpass the experience of Victoria Falls. Following the footpath from the hotel, hiking through the forest, one is deafened by the 'smoke that thunders,' rounding the last corner and seeing the Zambezi River plunging hundreds of feet over the rocks and down into the river bed. The falls have been captured on film, video, and by the stroke of the painters brush. But no renderings do it justice. Some things must be seen to be appreciated. I thought to myself, *Did God do this for fun? Is this type of thing His hobby? Or, is this simply another example of His wooing man to Himself?* G.K. Chesterton once said, 'If my children have Santa to thank for putting goodies in their stockings, whom do I have to thank for putting two feet into mine?'"[10]

"See, Sherri, in the same way that we woo those to whom we are attracted, God creates all that is beautiful in this world to woo us to Himself. God, Himself, seeks a relationship of love between the Creator and creature but does not violate free will to obtain it."

Nearing the end of her patience Sherri responded, "Once more, Jeff, what does this have to do with the suffering, pain, and evil in this world?" Calmly I gave response: "Love and free will are directly connected to the pain and suffering in this world. Love cannot occur without freedom, but freedom opens the door to all that is tragic in our world."

With every ear listening I continued, "Can you imagine the tension God must have encountered in His decision to create? He wanted love to be the highest value in His universe— love between Creator and creature, and between creature and creature. The only way, however, that God could ensure that every man and woman on the planet could receive and return such love, was to insert within every human being a microchip whereby He could control the mind of every person, determining that throughout every generation, all men and women would love God and love their neighbor as themselves. But wait! What is the problem with this scenario? Such love would be neither genuine nor authentic. Such robotic emotion where the giver and receiver have no choice cannot produce nor compel real love. Indeed, if love is the highest value in God's universe, the only way to ensure that such love exists is to replace the microchip of control with the microchip of free will! So, in the creation scenario, God grants free will in order to protect life's greatest pursuit and the world's highest value—love.

"Enter the tension! As soon as God decided to create a world where genuine, authentic love could exist, the potential for pain, suffering, and evil also became part of the package. Why? Essential to love is freedom. Freedom, however, can also result in the opposite—hate. Not everyone uses their free-will mechanism to do the honorable thing. Many choose not to pursue God or to love and protect one another. In fact, many choose to use their freedom for their own selfish purposes and their own self-aggrandizement. Instead of loving God and loving their neighbors as themselves, they would love themselves above all else and would use their freedom to advance their own purposes and plans in the world. This is what we know as 'self' love. Here is the punch line, Sherri. 'Self' love is the ultimate underlying characteristic and the primary motivation that catalyzes most of the suffering and pain in the world."

I noticed that both Sherri and Richard were captivated by this thought and were processing the implications. I attempted to drive the point even further.

"Sherri," I asked, "When someone says, 'Jeff, how could God create a place where there is suffering and pain?' What they are really asking is, 'How could God create a world that features the possibility of pain and suffering?' Few ever ask the question: 'How could God have ensured a world without pain?' Only one answer exists to that question, 'Create a world without free will and control every creature.' This is the only possible way to ensure that no pain, suffering, or evil exists in the creation scenario. Of course, in such a scenario love would not and could not exist either. But if that is the very reason the world was created, 'love' would be something that God would not be willing to sacrifice."

Time Out!

Recently, I had a conversation with a man in a café who was so angry that it became difficult to continue being logical. Frustrated that his arguments against God were going nowhere fast, he pointed his finger at me and said, "Look, Jeff, I will believe in God when He removes all the evil from this world!" My response? "OK, then you will be the first to go." Stunned, he sat back in his chair, slumped in defeat, and knew that his demand was logically impossible. As long as free-will men and women exist in this world, the potential for evil will always exist. The degree of pain and suffering will greatly depend upon the actions of free-will creatures.

See the point? If we want God to remove all the evil or the potential for evil from this world, then you and I will have to go as well. As long as humans with free will exist, there will always be the potential that such people will use their freedom (a freedom given in order that we would have the capability to love and be loved) to wreak havoc on one another. The real issue is: "Who is responsible for the pain and suffering in our world? God? Or is this simply man expressing his freedom in an inappropriate fashion?"

Into Africa

During the late eighties and early nineties this truth struck hard at the core of my belief system. Living in Zimbabwe and traveling regularly to what is referred to as the "bush" of Africa, I was constantly bombarded with poverty, hunger, and disease. Families in need of food, clothing, or shelter are not far from view. Confronted day after day with children whose bellies were swollen with hunger and malnutrition would cause anyone to raise his hands toward the heavens and complain, "God, how could you? Where are you? How could you create a world with such sadness and hopelessness, pain and suffering?"

It was in one of these moments that the reality of the situation came crashing down like a bolt of lightning. The cause of such injustice has very little to do with God. The real culprit lies once again in the free will of man. Any economist will tell you that it is not the absence of food and water that yields such horrible circumstances. No! It is the mismanagement of valuable resources which God has lovingly supplied.

Furthermore, due to the climatic conditions and the richness of Zimbabwean soil, this part of Africa is able to experience two growing seasons within only one twelve-month period. Although there are times of drought, there should never be times of famine. One year's harvest managed and distributed well, can feed the people of Zimbabwe for many years. Like many other African countries, God has supplied plenty!

So what is the issue? Why the food shortage? Why the hunger? Simply put: A man named Robert Mugabe is more interested in his own selfish pursuits and his own self-aggrandizement than in the welfare and safety of an entire nation of people. It is not my purpose to give a step-by-step description of how President Mugabe has depleted his country of valuable resources, sold those resources, and used the money for his own personal gain. This is not news to anyone. The fact that Mugabe is one of the richest men in the world, and that he continually sells food for foreign currency to other nations in order to stack his own bank account, is undeniable. Moreover, President Mugabe threatens those who oppose his regime with the promise to remove what little food is left if loyalty is not given to his party. What saddens me deeply is that the Shona people of Zimbabwe are some of the most pleasant people in the world. Unfortunately, they are also extremely passive.

What is the point of all of this? The old adage that "the Lord giveth and the Lord taketh away" is indeed true. *In the present world system, however, perhaps an even more appropriate statement is, "The Lord giveth and man taketh away."* The pain and suffering that exists in Zimbabwe has little to do with God (He has provided) and much to do with man. Human leaders often use their freedom to accomplish their own selfish agendas—agendas that often include the pain and suffering of their own people. Robert Mugabe comes from a long line of leaders who abuse their people and wreak havoc on a nation in order to pursue selfish gain. You and I see the starving children and the war-torn nations of people in poverty and run out into the street, throw our hands up in protest, and scream, "Why God?!" My guess is that God looks down in reply and lovingly states, "No, my friend; why, Man?" Indeed, why does man use his freedom, a freedom given in order that genuine and authentic love may exist in this creation scenario, to hurt and hate and punish one another?

Similarly, after the devastation of the 9/11 attacks appeared on every television set across America, people went into the churches of America and cried out, "God, how could you?" I am confident that God would look down and reply, "No, how could you? How could man use his freedom, given that he may love and pursue me and his fellow man, to wreak such havoc and commit such horrendous and dastardly deeds upon one another?" This seems to be man's pattern: Hitler, Lenin, Stalin, Saddam Hussein, and Osama Bin Laden; why does God get blamed for the actions of free-will creatures?

With Laura listening intently and the rest of the staff in deep consideration, I glanced over to Sherri and asked, "You want God to remove the possibility of all pain and suffering?" "Absolutely!" she responded.

"To do that, God would have to remove one of two things," I rebounded. "First, He could remove humanity from the earth. This may be effective but in one sense would be a greater evil. We are talking about widespread annihilation! Second, He could remove freedom, but if He removes freedom, the possibility of genuine love no longer exists. Since this is the very reason God made us in the first place, such a scenario seems high unlikely."

Silence of the Lambs

I wish you could have been there to experience the depth of contemplation taking place around the table. Dan was thinking about evil and good. Sherri visibly softened, considered the free-will argument. Others around the table dealt with their own issues, and, Richard, as well as every other male around the table, found it difficult to give up the hope that this computer chip might possibly exist.

Then there was Laura. She became emotional, constantly fought back tears and desperately tried to maintain control. Not knowing Laura, I wondered if perhaps she had been struck by some recent tragedy and all the talk about pain and suffering had reopened the wound. The silence was deafening.

A Quick Application

The search for significance is perhaps our greatest quest. I have never met anyone who simply wants to "take up space" on this planet. Most people really want, in fact need, to feel that their lives matter, that there is something outside of, and bigger than, themselves. This need to find the greater purpose for which I live—a purpose greater than just manipulating the world to revolve around me and my desires and mandates—needs to be examined. From where does it come? We are often told that our value is directly related to that in which we invest our lives. This is why we give, rightly or wrongly, greater respect to the president than we do to the postal worker. In our minds, the purpose for which the president lives is of greater significance. Both are important, but the latter possesses greater potential for affecting lives.

I once heard a speaker challenge the audience that he could take a bar of steel and considerably alter its value by changing the purpose for which it was used. He emphatically stated,

> If I took a bar of steel and I made it into 16 penny nails; that bar of steel would be worth about $60 or so. But if I take this bar of steel and I invest it into sewing needles, this bar of steel

---

will now be worth about $300. But instead of nails or needles, let's say we invest this bar of steel in cutlery or knife blades. This bar of steel will now be worth about $3,000. But say, instead of cutlery or knife blades, instead of needles or nails, we invest this same bar of steel into very fine Swiss watch springs. That bar of steel will now be worth over two million dollars. What changed its worth? What it was invested in.[11]

In the deepest regions of the heart resides the undeniable desire for significance.

Once again, from where does such a desire come? I believe that it is highly tenable to suggest that God, wanting beyond all other things, a love relationship with the creation, placed within every human heart this desire for significance. How is the thirst for significance related to our choice to love God?

Remember, God cannot force love, He can only compel it. What better way to woo us to Himself than to create us with a built-in need that only He can satisfy?

God's hope is that when we have tried every temporary means to fill this eternal need, we will finally seek Him with all our hearts. At this point, the reason we live dramatically transforms and the value of our lives significantly increases. Not only do I matter; I matter to the God of this universe! I have been made for a purpose! I am part of a plan! There is a role that only I can fill!

Therefore, we must come to the point where we are willing to ask two questions. One, is that in which I am investing my life yielding temporary fruit that, like the grass in the field, is here today and gone tomorrow? Or, is that for which I am living my life paying dividends that will last for eternity? Living for a purpose that transcends the temporary is a powerful and effective way to live and gives an indescribable sense of worth to the person who chooses such a path.

Second, we must inquire as to the origin of this desire for significance. Where does the desire come from in the first place? Why do we feel the need to matter? Who placed this desire within every human heart?

Once again, the answer is found in the question. Only the Creator of all things, the One who has access to each of our hearts, is capable of creating this universal desire. This is one of the ways that God draws us unto Himself without violating our freedom. He places what Pascal calls a "God-shaped" void that only He can fill.

In other words, there are some things for which the human heart longs that no earthly thing can completely fill. Perhaps God's plan is that when we come to this realization, that the temporary cannot fill the eternal, pure logic will move us toward the eternal God. Perhaps Augustine was right: "Our souls are restless until we find our rest in Him."

Chapter Three

Yearning for a Better Planet!

8:10 P.M. and still hungry . . .

*A*ll the free food I had hoped to eat had not been touched. Aware that it was now growing cold on my plate, I reached down to savor a few warm bites. Suddenly, a young lady in her mid-twenties, sitting two places down from Dan, decided she had held her tongue long enough. So Jucinda bellowed, "Jeff, I will confess that you've got us thinking, but you seem to forget one very important issue. *Man's freedom is not the cause of all the pain and suffering in this world.* What about earthquakes, floods, and other natural disasters? Does man's free will cause the death and devastation of those who are killed by such horrific events?"

As though he had been given new life, Dan perked up as if to say, "Yeah! What she said!"

A Quick Summary

Remember, while Dan questioned, although illogically, the existence of God, Sherri questioned the goodness of God in relation to all the pain and suffering in the world. We have shown how Dan's question cannot be asked unless an Absolute Moral Lawgiver is assumed. Again, his question is self-defeating. Without God there is no such thing as absolute evil.

Sherri's question, however, is a fair and logical query. If God is "good" then why did He create a scenario that featured the potential for such evil and badness? The answer of course resides in the value God places on love, and His intention to protect its integrity in the known universe. Again, the only logical way to provide an opportunity for genuine love is to grant human free will. The real problem rests not with God but with man and the manner in which he uses his freedom.

Jucinda, however, introduces yet another category: How could God just sit by and watch thousands of people die in natural disasters? What man's free will causes the explosion of volcanoes, the rushing of violent flood waters, the quaking of earth's foundations, and the sudden impact of hurricanes, tornadoes, and tsunamis?

Unlike that of Dan and Sherri, Jucinda's tone exposed a sincere hope that a satisfactory answer could be given. Not privy to any conspiracy, she just wanted answers. She reminded me of someone who was contemplating suicide but genuinely wanted to be talked out of it. "Give me hope. I want to believe in God, but how can I when He is so violent?" Although she did not say these exact words, her facial expressions and body language revealed her struggle. Taking a chance, I asked her if I could tell her a story that might clarify the issue for all of us. "Please," she replied. With Laura looking more and more emotionally distraught, I shared a secret with Jucinda that I had never shared with anyone before.

"When I was younger, I greatly admired my older brother. He never knew this and would probably be shocked to read this today. Nevertheless, he was everything I wanted to be:

strong, muscular, handsome, and confident. I remember an incident as we walked down the hallway at school. Suddenly, a boy much larger in stature raised his leg in a karate move and struck my brother in the jaw. To this day I do not know why he treated my brother in such a way. I just remember that within seconds my big brother Timothy pinned the culprit to a locker in one of his infamous wrestling moves and commanded him to beg for mercy. I did not hear all that was said but as I watched this young man run away in fear, respect and adoration for Timothy significantly increased! I remember thinking, *"Wow! My big brother is the strongest most feared boy in school. You don't mess around with Tim!"*

"Imagine my confusion a few years later when one of my brother's best friends physically and verbally threatened me while Tim sat idly by. In my mind it was the greatest treason. My brother had both the power and the love to stop this torture, yet, he did nothing."

I asked Jucinda if this was a good summary of her position. "Absolutely," she said. "Why does God sit idly by during the destruction caused by a tsunami? God has the power to prevent all natural disasters. How then, could He stand by while the devastation occurs and innocent people suffer unimaginable sorrow?"

Secular Man's Oxymoron

Before attempting to resolve this conflict, I asked Jucinda to consider the irony in all of this. The secular man will put on his scientific hat, go to a meeting, and deliver a paper discussing how man's abuse of this planet is causing all kinds of destruction. Global warming, holes in the ozone, floods, famines, droughts, and the like are all attributed to man's irresponsible handling of earth's resources. The postmodern man screams in protest at big businesses and superpowers that exude apathy and refuse to treat the creation responsibly. Then, in what must seem like the greatest hypocritical move of all time, the secular man changes his clothes, goes to a philosophical meeting, and leads a discussion that denounces and debunks God on the basis of all the bad things (earthquakes, floods, volcano eruptions) that are happening in the world.

In one sense, blaming God for the condition of the planet is similar to a child leaving his new bicycle outside in the rain for six months and then blaming God for the rust! It is not beyond logic to point out that when we abuse what God has given to us, bad things happen. The pursuit of power serves as the basis for all destruction. The only foolproof way to stop the abuse that leads to the demise of our planet is to remove man's freedom to choose. Yes, God could order a universe where humans always make the right decisions; however, while removing our freedom might protect the planet, it would destroy the ultimate goal of creation: genuine, authentic love.

After explaining this to Jucinda, a glimmer of hope seemed to twinkle in her eye. Perhaps this issue was not as difficult as she once thought. Maybe this free-will issue is much bigger than any of us could imagine. I knew, however, that there were plenty of holes in my argument, and that if I had any real hope of encouraging Jucinda beyond today and into tomorrow, much more needed to be said.

8:30 P.M. round the table we go . . .

A Familiar Story

The tsunami of 2004 left a path of destruction in its wake. On December 27th, the day after, all the major news networks (CNN, BBC, MSNBC, ABC, CBS, NBC, and FOX) plastered pictures of death and devastation on television screens all over the world. Tens of thousands of people lost their lives, loved ones, and their homes. A geophysicist compared the force of the quake that catalyzed the tsunami with a million atomic bombs dropped during World War II. The power was so intense that it actually interrupted the rotation of the earth.

Most of us are not geophysicists and were not primarily concerned that the earth's rotation was momentarily interrupted. This bit of information, although interesting, did not become our focal point. As people who place value on people, we were more concerned that lives were interrupted in such a way that, for many, things would never be the same. Days after the tsunami hit, front page newspapers all over the world featured captions that asked, "Why?" Coming from the atheistic media and other organizations that denounce the possibility of a moral universe, this was surprising. Most of the photos focused on little children because we often associate children with innocence. When something bad happens to a child, we think of injustice. "What could that child possibly have done to deserve this?" we complain. Even in New Zealand, a completely and unashamedly secular country, a man named Satya Kumari was featured on the front page of the December 28th edition of *The [New Zealand] Herald*. Under Mr. Kumari's photo, the caption, in big black letters, read: "What did we do to deserve this? Why did the children have to die? Why are there so many people who have been stripped of their hopes and dreams?"

While many sympathize with these questions and, indeed, feel the pain of those who have suffered, others use such events as ammunition, loading their argumentative guns, as they wait for the dust to settle. They can hardly wait to fire their philosophical bullets toward those who affirm the existence of God. "Why," they ask, "if God exists, is there suffering in this world?"

Here is where the rubber hits the road! Although the question is indeed a fair one, and one that needs serious contemplation, be aware that such a question assumes two things. First, it assumes that suffering is a "bad" or "evil" thing. C.S.

Lewis said, *"We do not merely posit the reality of pain. We position the question in a decidedly moral category."*[12]

"Jucinda," I said, "you are asking why God allows these events to occur because you believe that He is good and a tsunami is evil and the two should not coexist, correct?"

"Yes," she responded.

"Well," I said, "this is the problem for the one who denounces God; this is where they undermine their own thinking. Once we denounce the absolute categories of 'good' and 'evil,' we forfeit the right to label any event in human history as categorically 'good' or 'bad.' The secularist proclaims that 'Moral law is left up to the individual.' This may sound good, but in reality it is anything but good. After all, in the mind of some people, the tsunami was a 'good' thing. I heard one man say, *'The world is overpopulated. The illiterate poor need to go in order to make room for the better educated citizens who will make significant contributions to human progression!'*"

You should have seen the disgust on my hosts' faces.

I continued, "My secular humanist friends would be outraged at such a statement. But upon what grounds could they argue the point? Upon what basis could they claim that such a statement was corrupt?"

Jucinda interrupted, "What are you talking about? Of course such a statement is pathetic and bigoted."

"Wait a minute!" I said. "When morality is left up to the individual, what happens when two moral laws, which directly oppose one another, collide? Who is to determine who is 'right' and who is 'wrong'?"

What Is the Point?

The point is that as soon as we denounce "absolute moral law," we lose the right to postulate a question that assumes it. Yet this is exactly what occurs in the public arena everyday. Whether on television or in the halls of academia, we ask, "How can you believe in God when there is so much suffering in the world?" while at the same time denying the categories of absolute "good" and "evil." Jucinda's question, just like Dan's, assumes "suffering" is categorically and absolutely evil, otherwise, the question would have no bite! Yes, we have the right to ask why God allows natural disasters, but in doing so, we assume His existence. Let us not forget that.

Second, the question, "Why did this happen?" assumes purpose and reason to the universe. Logically speaking however, if there is no Creator and we are all here by some cosmic accident, then, indeed not only is there no absolute moral law, but neither is there any reason for any event that ever occurs. As harsh as it may seem, the tsunami of 2004, if God is debunked, was nothing more than one group of chemicals covering another group of chemicals in order to weed out the weak so that the strong may survive.

Remember the slogan of the atheistic evolutionist, "Evolution is red in tooth and claw." Blood will be spilled, but it's all in the name of a mindless progression or evolution. This tsunami, in a very natural sense, is the earth shedding unwanted chemicals (*including people*) to evolve into the next stage; to make way for stronger and more resilient chemicals! This is a good thing, a productive thing! Right?

This sort of devaluing of humanity has been around for a long time and can still be seen in postmodern philosophies of life. Deepak Chopra, the latest eastern guru who markets eastern pantheism with western materialism, words it like this:

> *On the material level, both you and a tree are made up of the same recycled elements, mostly carbon, hydrogen, oxygen, nitrogen and other elements in minute amounts. You can buy these elements in a hardware store for a couple of dollars. The difference between the two of you is in the energy and the information. Your body is not separated from the body of the universe. Because of the quantum mechanical levels there are no well-defined edges. You are like a wig-*

gle, a wave, a fluctuation, a convolution, a whirlpool, a localized disturbance, in the larger quantum field.[13]

My question is a simple one: If we are not greater in value than chemicals purchased at a hardware store and higher in worth than the other energies found in the universe, then what is the big problem when a tsunami occurs? I am sure the other wiggles, waves, and convolutions do not ask the "why?" question when something tragic happens. In fact, I am positive that such elements do not have the capacity to do so.

According to Chopra, "there are no well-defined edges." He is not sure where a tree stops and I start. Yet, the tree could never write these words or ask these questions. Maybe, just maybe, the soul and the mind have something to say about all this. The point remains, if we are nothing more than accidental chemicals bouncing to and fro, this is a purposeless universe with no plan or reason. In such a universe, the "why" question becomes illogical. Yet, the "why" question prevails as if it has been intrinsically planted into the heart and mind of every person who has ever lived. The fact that we have the ability to ask, "Why?" should alert us to the fact that we are special, unique, and purposefully placed.

The atheist, however, by reducing us to cosmic accidents, has forfeited his right to ask "why" concerning anything. So the questions, Why is there suffering in the world? Why did the children have to die? are self-defeating questions. Tsunamis are simply chemicals accidentally moving and shuffling around from one place to another. There is no method to the madness! No reason exists!

Jucinda's Fire Reignited

Introducing Jucinda to these issues reignited her passion. With Laura continuing to look distressed and on the verge of an outburst, Jucinda chimed in with her next accusation. "Jeff," she demanded, "you said we have the right to ask why. I am asking. Why would this good and loving and all-powerful God, about whom you are speaking, allow such a tragedy to take place? Answer your own question! Why doesn't He stop these disasters?"

I was tempted to jump immediately into providing a logical, plausible solution to this great dilemma. However, I knew that before an answer could be given and accepted, a warning needed to be issued. When I mentioned this to Jucinda she responded, "What kind of warning?" I asked her to reconsider that when the great tsunami struck Asia, philosophers came out from behind the bushes with their atheistic bullets wishing to assassinate the "God-botherers"[14] in their midst. There was one man however, Garth George, a regular columnist for *The New Zealand Herald*, who took an interesting approach to the subject. Not wanting to debunk nor defend God he wrote:

> *A lot of far greater minds than mine have pronounced at great length on the age-old conundrum of pain and suffering, and none has ever got much further than the inevitable conclusion, "We don't know."*[15]

In one respect, George is correct. Who can fathom the mind, the work, and the doings of God? One of my daughter's favorite activities is to bombard me with a series of "why" questions. Why is the sky blue? Why is the grass green? Why does a cow go moo? Why does a dog bark? On and on and on it goes! As she gets older, however, the questions become more and more complex. Why do babies come from mommy's tummy? Why does my brother always pick his nose? Why do you have to go to work every day? These make for great conversation pieces, but in reality although many of her questions have logical, sensible solutions, her mind is not yet ready to take hold of the answers.

Parents recognize that they can save a lot of time by simply giving the standard answer—"Because I said so"—to difficult questions. It is not that no answer exists, it is simply that it would take too long and require a greater capacity of understanding than the child presently maintains. An answer could be given but it would not be understood.

I have experienced this same dilemma with our family dog Milo. To this day, Milo thinks that a chocolate cake covered neatly on the kitchen counter is a direct invitation for him to stand on his hind legs, remove the covering, and devour the goods. No other food item causes such a reaction. Funny thing is, no matter how many times I try to communicate to Milo that the chocolate cake is for humans and not dogs, he doesn't seem to take it in. In his mind, this is gourmet dog food prepared especially for him. Thus, a communication gap exists to which I have found no bridge. Now, if a difference in the capacity of understanding exists between Milo and me, and between my daughter and me, how much more so between God and me?

This line of reasoning prompted Jucinda to respond, "What a cop out!" To put her mind at ease I assured her that this idea alone was in no way a sufficient answer to such a difficult question. I reminded her that I was merely pointing out that Garth George had a valid point. If we could exhaustively grasp every facet of creation, then, would we not be God ourselves?

In fact, as humans we accept so many things in our lives for which we do not have a complete nor exhaustive understanding. Take the example of one of the most famous stories ever written; it is the story in the Bible about a man named Job. He was a man who experienced more pain and suffering than you and I could ever imagine. As a picture of his true humanity, Job did not suffer quietly. Question after question rose from his lips in an attempt to understand how a good God could allow so much pain in the life of someone who had been blameless. (See Job 1:1.) After a long series of demands and questions, in a classic piece of literature, God breaks His silence and responds with a series of His own questions:

Who is this that darkens my counsel
   with words without knowledge?

Brace yourself like a man;
> I will question you,
> and you shall answer me.
>> (Job 38:2-3)

Where were you when I laid the earth's foundation?
> Tell me, if you understand.
Who marked off its dimensions? Surely you know!

Have you journeyed to the springs of the sea
> or walked in the recesses of the deep?
Have the gates of death been shown to you?

What is the way to the abode of light?
> And where does darkness reside?

Can you bring forth the constellations in their seasons?

Who endowed the heart with wisdom
> or gave understanding to the mind?

Do you know when the mountain goats give birth?
> Do you watch when the doe bears her fawn?
>> (Job 38:4-5a,16-17a,19,32a,36; 39:1)

What is God implying? Job had built his entire argument on the premise that he would be able to endure all the pain, if he were granted comprehensive knowledge of his suffering. God was simply reminding Job that there were many things in his life he readily accepted (dimensions of the earth, depth of the sea, source of heavenly lights, processes of life and death) without possessing a complete or exhaustive understanding.[16]

If God were to make readily available a complete explanation of the reasons He allows difficulties to enter our lives, chances are, in the same way that my two-year-old son could not understand what I meant by "it will ruin your appetite" when denying him ice cream, so also, would God need to qualify every term and condition before we could categorically begin to comprehend the plans of the infinite.

However, to suggest that we know nothing about God's workings and doings in the midst of tsunamis and other natural disasters, is just as erroneous as suggesting we know everything. With eyes once again glued in my direction I asked the group to consider a logical, plausible, and tenable answer to the question: How could a good, loving God allow the tsunamis of our world?

The Answer Was Given Long Ago

Way back in first-century Rome a man named Paul wrote a letter to a group of people totally committed to God. However, they were struggling with the concept of an all-powerful, all-loving Creator who permitted a creation-scenario that included storms, floods, earthquakes, and the like. Why would a loving God allow such catastrophes? Paul's answer is interesting to say the least. He reminds them that "The creation was subjected to frustration, not by its own choice, but by the will of the one who subjected it" (Romans 8:20 in the Bible).

The Greek word translated "frustration" (in some versions translated "futility") is *mataiotes* which means, *unable to achieve an original goal.* Paul assumes that because the creation did not achieve its original goal, it has now been subjected to a secondary, yet no less important, objective. Therefore, this "subjection to futility" has occurred in the hope that something higher and more significant would take place.

The questions are: What was God's original goal in creation? Why was this goal not achieved? What is the new goal of creation?

By insinuation Paul suggests that when God created the world, he never designed it to produce earthquakes, volcanoes, and tsunamis. Instead, motivated by the desire to draw all men and women into a relationship, God supplied a beautiful, wondrous, and perfect world which man could live in and enjoy. All that man needed was provided. From the shiny red apple to the thundering waterfall, God shed His grace on man. This line of reasoning is consistent with the Genesis account that describes how the world began.

The next question, however, is, why did God give so many wonderful gifts in the original creation scenario? As discussed above, the answer is love. God, without violating free will, gave wonderful and majestic gifts to man so that he might use his freedom to express gratitude to the Creator and yearn to enter into an intimate relationship with the One who loves him in the way that he seeks to be loved.

Instead of expressing love and gratitude, however, men and women (the creatures) rebelled against God, choosing to go their own way, loving themselves and their ambitions more than the One who had given them so much. In fact, they began to place more worth on the created than the Creator. Is this really hard to believe? Has anything really changed since then? Our drive and desire to chase and pursue material things significantly overrides any desire we might have to worship and give glory to the eternal God for all the good things that exist in our world; mountains, streams, lakes, oceans, planets, etc.

Knowing man's response, God subjected the creation to frustration, altering its primary objective. What is that new objective? To show man that placing one's faith in the creation, which is temporary, is an eternal mistake. Love is still the highest value in the universe, and God's greatest goal is to woo us to Himself. However, to woo us to Himself, God first of all must now woo us away from the creation with which we are so enamored. Creation, as beautiful and wonderful as it is, was never meant to be the ultimate object of our affection. The creation is temporary. To remind us of this, God subjects it to frustration so that from time to time it raises its ugly head and reminds all of us that, along with the rest of humanity, creation is in decay and will one day meet its maker and be restored to original glory (see Romans 8:21).

Knowing that these ideas were difficult to grasp, I asked Jucinda and her companions to tolerate two quick illustrations that I believed would solidify the point.

A Day at the Beach!

Some time ago, on a nice summer morning, my wife and I took the kids for a stroll down Mairangi Bay beach. This lovely beach on Auckland, New Zealand's North Shore is perfect for building sand castles. While Robin and I put our heads back on the blanket, thanking God that our children were now old enough to take care of themselves, the children set about doing their typically favorite beach activities. Delaney, our ten-year-old son, spent the morning skipping rocks, while Sian, our people-pleasing eight-year old, set about the task of building the proverbial sand castle city! Majestic, detailed, and pleasant to the eye, our daughter had created a masterpiece. Upon completing the endeavor, she ran as fast as she could to wake her comfortably snoozing father to show him this outstanding accomplishment. Deciding to use this as a great opportunity to teach Sian a valuable lesson, I responded in a way that shook her little world. Seeing this incredible edifice surrounded by a precious little mote, I began verbally pondering how such a thing could ever have come into existence. "Wow!" I said, "Look Sian, while we were sleeping last night the tide formed this beautiful city of sand! The wind and the waves pushed and shoved the sand into the precise manner in which to form this beautiful, wonderful, and majestic structure. Truly, this is a masterpiece!"

She stood and stared at me as if I had lost my mind, then angrily screamed in protest, "No Dad! I built this! I made this! Can't you see? I did it! Oh, Daddy!" Severely disappointed that she had not received praise from her father, she marched off toward her mother in search of comfort.

Presents under the Tree

This same lovely little girl believed in Santa Claus right up until she was almost nine-years-old. While most children her age had long dismissed the jolly old elf, Sian refused to denounce his royal redness! In the eighth year of her existence, however, she began to demand answers. Every Christmas the presents under the tree were gladly and energetically appreciated as Sian, holding her presents in hand, danced around the tree with a grateful heart. Not wanting this joy to come to an end, I went to great lengths to prolong the façade. From eating the cookies left for Santa to sprinkling red glitter on the deck of our home as proof Santa's sleigh had been there, no masquerade was too great to prolong a grateful heart. Year after year the presents came. Year after year Sian's gratitude increased. Until one day Sian walked into my office and said, "Dad, I want to meet Santa."

"What do you mean?" I asked. "I take you to the mall every year to sit on his lap and tell him what you want."

"No, Dad. I know those men are not the real Santa. I want to meet the real man!"

"Why?" I asked.

The answer I received was unexpected, "Because I want to thank the one who has given me so much!"

Following these two precious little stories I asked Jucinda to consider something very crucial to our journey. First, in the sand-castle story, did Sian have the right to expect a little praise from her father for what she had accomplished? What decent father would not congratulate his daughter who, motivated out of providing pleasure for her father's eyes, spent the time and effort necessary to create such a masterpiece?

Second, in the Santa story, can it not be said that the natural response to receiving wonderful gifts is gratitude? Should God not expect praise and gratitude for all the good He has given us?

A Final Illustration

When I was a little boy, spending Christmas at Grandma and Grandpa's was undoubtedly the highlight of the year. My three brothers and I looked forward with great anticipation to the traditional Christmas Eve celebration, where we would open the presents from our grandparents who would spare no expense to put a smile on the grandchildren's faces. One particular Christmas remains very special to me because it was the Christmas when I began to truly understand what this giving and receiving thing was all about. My grandparents had placed the gifts under the tree uncharacteristically early one year. In fact, the gifts had been bought and wrapped as early as Thanksgiving Day. With more than a month until Christmas Eve, my brothers and I found this to be almost unbearable. Every trip to Grandpa's house included a ten-to fifteen-minute adventure of shaking and rattling these presents in an attempt to discover the secret contents. To make matters worse, hidden away in the corner was a huge gift with my name on it. This was the tallest present I had ever seen, and, it was mine, all mine! For more than thirty days, this one particular present was the topic of conversation at dinner time. The fact that my brothers reeked with jealousy was overshadowed only by the arrogance and pride at which I approached every new day. "I have the biggest present," I would remind them. "Grandma and Grandpa obviously love me the most!" This shameless pride grew until Christmas Eve issued in the time to open presents. With sheer force and reckless abandonment I tore into the box only to discover it was empty! Over four feet of wadded up newspaper and other types of confetti brought an inexplicable disappointment. I wept. Soon, however, I learned that this was no prank. My grandparents had simply chosen this route to ensure that the joy I would experience in discovering the real gift would be the highest possible form of ecstasy. Down deep in the very bottom of the box lay a note that read, 'Dear Jeff, go look under Grandpa's bed.' With a hope beyond all hope I sprinted to Grandpa's room, lifted the blanket, and peered into the dark, as I waited for my eyes to adjust. When my sight returned, I saw the biggest, brightest, reddest "Red Ryder" sled I had ever seen! It had all the bells and whistles too! I knew I was going to have a winter like no other. I jumped and shouted and screamed out in gratitude and appreciation for what had been given to me. It was then that I saw the look in my Grandfather's eye that I will never forget.

His pleasure seemed greater than mine. How could that be? I was the one who received the gift. He was the one who made great sacrifices to obtain the treasure and then give it away. My grandfather, for most of his life, worked on an assembly line and made just enough money to survive. Young as I might be, even then, I understood the great sacrifice he had made. Yet, I had never seen my grandfather more content and at peace with the world than on that night when he selflessly gave to someone else. It was then and there that I began to understand the concept that it is more blessed to give than receive. When it came to gratitude, I saved Grandpa for last. I ran to him, looked up, smiled, and said, "That's the best present I ever got, Grandpa." I thought he was going to cry. I had been drawn to my grandfather in a very special way. More importantly, however, even at this young age I wondered to myself, *If my grandfather receives so much pleasure in giving gifts to his grandchildren, how much more does the Heavenly Father feel such pleasure when He gives gifts to His children?*

Bringing It All Together

The point is that God immensely enjoys giving to His creatures. Yet His common graces are not the end in themselves. They have a purpose. From the wonders of the world to the smallest pleasures of life, this creation was originally designed to compel man to seek this good and gracious God who has provided so much enjoyment in His creation scenario.

In other words, all has been provided in order that the Provider might be desired, sought, and communed with. This is what God desires more than anything else. Love is the highest value of this universe, and community in relationship between Creator and creature is the ultimate goal.

Dan had been silent for some time now, so I decided to draw him back into the conversation by returning to his original argument. Like a groundhog cautiously raising his head above the surface for fear he may see his shadow, Dan, when asked to consider again the logical conclusion of his argument, glanced slowly and carefully in my direction.

If the presence of evil in the world casts God's existence into doubt, then, alternatively, does the presence of so much goodness not affirm it? Indeed, think of all the good in your life; in most lives, the good far outweighs the bad. And before one plays the "poor African" card again, let me remind you that the Shona people of Zimbabwe, even in the midst of their poverty, are some of the happiest people I know. The simple pleasures of life are often embraced in gratitude by those who are not spoiled and who have not yet come to expect that life should be all joy and no pain. The point is that while pain may be present in this world, joy reigns abundant within every individual life. Pleasures abound in this creation scenario. The question is, "Why?" Why has God given so much pleasure? From the act of marriage in matrimonial bliss to the gentle hugs and kisses of daddy's little girl, why so much pleasure?

Our Response, God's Tension

Remember, from God's perspective, the oceans, lakes, mountains, streams, and every other wonder in the world have been intentionally designed to woo the creature into a loving relationship with the Creator. This allows God to make the first move toward us without violating our free will. Unfortunately, like the first man and woman, instead of seeking God in gratitude, man seems intent upon glorifying himself or worshiping the creation. Think about it. The foundation upon which most, if not all, philosophies of the modern world are built includes the belief that man is the result of some cosmic accident with no real purpose or meaning. Quite humorous are the efforts made by the secular ethicists to come up with moral theories in such an accidental world. At any rate, that which was designed to compel the human heart toward gratitude has instead been relegated to the category of accidental, therefore requiring nothing more than superficial acknowledgement and a "man, aren't we lucky" attitude.

Instead of expressing thoughts of gratitude and placing our faith ultimately in the Creator, we turn our attention and give our allegiance to the created thing itself. This of course makes no logical sense. It is the equivalent of admiring a beautiful painting to the degree that the painter is forgotten and the colors on the canvas become the focal point of all praise. Is it not logical to ask, "Where is the painter?" "Can I meet him that I may shake his hand?"

What could a God, who values love and relationship above all things, do to draw men to Himself, without violating free will? There is only one answer: reveal to man the ramifications of placing one's hope and trust in the created rather than the Creator. Man must realize that only the Creator is eternal and dependable. The moment man places all his hope and faith in what is temporal, namely the creation, the tide will come in and wash all your hopes and dreams away. True, the creation is wonderful and beautiful, but it is not to be worshiped because, like the painting, it is a reflection of something or someone else.

The point is that worshiping the creation will ultimately destroy you. Your hopes, dreams, and future are contingent upon the longevity of that upon which you place your trust.

Place your faith in what will one day fade away, and you too will one day experience the ultimate defeat. Alternatively, place your hope and trust on that which is eternal, and yours will be a victorious life with a positive future.

The truth is that if God is really love and genuinely wants what is best for the creature, *how could He stand by and watch the whole world place their hope and trust in what is temporary when He has something eternal to give?* I suggest to you that He cannot and does not. So, without violating free will, He has subjected this creation scenario to futility in the hope that it will achieve a higher purpose.

The Crux of the Matter

We said earlier that the Greek word for futility is *mataiotes* which means: "unable to achieve an original goal." The original purpose of creation was to point us to the Creator. Man refused to acknowledge God, so, although the creation is still wonderful and beautiful, God has subjected it to futility. In other words, it will not last forever. It is temporary. It is passing. And if you place your faith and trust in this creation scenario, sooner or later the storms of life will hit and reveal how temporary this world really is.

Moreover, we said earlier that God does this in hope. In hope for what? In hope that when man is reminded how temporary this world really is, he will place his faith in what is eternal, namely, the God of the universe. When man seeks the painter not the painted, he will be restored. In short, to inspire men to seek the eternal is the reason God has subjected the creation to frustration.

Are We Hypocrites?

Before you are so quick to rebuke God for allowing evil into the world, remember that almost every parent engages in a similar activity. Every father knows the value of allowing or even causing a painful event in order to thwart a greater and more intense evil. Whenever a child engages in behavior that has the potential to destroy him, no loving, caring parent would stand idly by and watch the child destroy himself. When my father caught me smoking a cigarette, he took away my weekend privileges. If he had caught me taking drugs, I would imagine the punishment to be a bit more dramatic. The point is that the greater the potential for destruction the more intense the level of prevention. Does God, as the Creator of all things, not possess this privilege? Within every earthquake, every flood, and every tsunami the voice of God shouts out to humanity, "Stop placing your faith in what is temporary. Draw near to God and He will draw near to you and give you what cannot be shaken" (see Hebrews 10:1-25).

9:20 P.M. encircling the issues . . .

Incomplete Answers

"Jeff, are you saying that God sent this tsunami which killed tens of thousands of people so that the rest of us would understand the futility of dethroning the Creator and replacing him with created things?" Jucinda complained.

"If you are asking me if God had a board meeting in heaven on the 26th of December and suggested that a tsunami be sent as a warning sign to the rest of the world, then my answer is 'no.'" I responded. "God's hand in any world disaster can be likened to His role in an outdoor wedding in New Zealand that is ruined by rain."

"What do you mean?" asked Jucinda.

"Performing outdoor weddings in Auckland, New Zealand, is a risky task." I said. "'Four seasons is one day' is an accurate description of the climate in Auckland." Being fully aware of this, many still choose to hold their wedding celebrations outdoors—something I will never understand. I remember one elderly lady who was getting married. She approached me with high hopes and begged me to pray my best prayer in order that it might not rain on her wedding day. I assured her that I would and I did. The wedding day came, and . . . it rained! It rained hard!

We scurried indoors and did our best to keep everything, especially the food, from getting wet. After the wedding festivities were completed, my elderly friend came to me and asked, "Why, Jeff? Why did it rain on my wedding day?" Pausing for a moment, knowing that she would take it well, I responded by saying, "Well, all this moisture formed over the Tasman Sea and moved inland and dumped the water onto the land where your wedding just happened to be." In other words, it rained because that's what God designed the earth to do from the beginning. The sun draws the moisture, and when the clouds hold all they can hold, only one thing can happen—rain. I don't think God made a decision to send rain upon your wedding day. Instead, your wedding day just happened to be on the same day that the clouds were due to release their moisture in what we call "precipitation." After I completed my practical dissertation, she smiled, nodded, and said, "I get your point."

This is a point I wish that many others would understand. The Creator of the universe, long before the tsunami ever struck, placed within the creation scenario a glitch whereby the temporariness of this world would express itself from time to time. No one knows when the times will be. In the same way that a cloud bursts when it is full of water, volcanoes erupt when they are full of heat, and the earth moves when the pressure becomes uncontainable, so also do tsunamis strike when waters are moved. Since we do not possess infinite knowledge, it is difficult to know for certain if a tsunami is the result of man's abuse of this planet or the ramifications of God's secondary goal for the universe He created. Whether tragedies appear through allowance or causation, God's goal is that tsunami-

---

type events push us away from the temporary and compel us toward the eternal.

From an individual perspective, the real issue is, "When the tsunamis of life come, upon what or whom have I placed my hope?" Am I trusting in the temporary or the eternal? This is life's most penetrating question. After all, sooner or later, we are all struck by some tragedy that leads to death. Upon what or whom will we place our faith?

Still interacting with Jucinda, I asked her if things were beginning to make sense. She responded, "Yes, for the most part, but I am still struggling with why God would even create men and women knowing that they may use their freedom to rebel and to wreak havoc on one another. You will have to admit, Jeff, that the risk is so high!"

Although her point was well made, she needed to see once again how we as humans engage in the very same practice and think it honorable. This practice is called parenthood.

Great Expectations

When my son Delaney was born it was truly one of the happiest days of my life. I stood in the hospital corridor in Cincinnati, Ohio, and peered through the window at this little bundle of joy. I began to think of all the possibilities. Surely a son of mine would discover a cure for cancer, build rocket ships that go to the moon, and manufacture a method to cure world hunger. All of this before his tenth birthday of course! In my mind, the opportunities and possibilities were endless. But then, as the cold winter air rushed in through an unclosed window, my mind began to wander down a road with which I was extremely uncomfortable. I thought of men like Hitler, Stalin, Jeffery Dahmer, and Ted Bundy. What if my son turned out to be one of those guys? I had read enough to know that some of the most hateful and evil people had parents who tried their best to love, teach, and nurture their child, but to no avail. In fact, my mind went back to Dr. James Dobson's interview with Ted Bundy, the noted serial killer. Dobson, a committed Christian, wanted to know what made Bundy tick. As a spokesman for effective parenthood, Dobson could give parents everywhere systematic advice concerning things to avoid when raising children. What he discovered was a man who had every chance of making the right choices. Good parents, good role models, and relatives who had pointed the child in the right direction.

The point is that every parent who decides to procreate does so with great risk. There are no guarantees in this life. The child could grow up to be president of the United States, or he could grow up to be a Robert Mugabe-type dictator whose life is consumed with his own selfish agenda with no care or concern for others. He could cure cancer thereby saving thousands upon thousands of lives, or he could become a serial killer, taking the lives of others and forever wounding the lives of those left behind.

True, there are many things parents can do to give the child the greatest chance of succeeding, but in the end, this little mechanism called "free will" kicks in and the choices the child makes will greatly affect who the child becomes. No doubt, parenthood is a great risk. So then, why take it? Simple. Love is the highest value in this universe and, other than the love of God for His people and the love of a husband for his wife or wife for her husband, no greater love exists. Most fathers and mothers would be more than willing to die for their children. The potential for this immeasurable love relationship between parent and child is enough to encourage the mothers and fathers of this world to bear children. The enormous potential for deep love, tremendous joy, and great meaning far outweighs any fear that the child may reject them and go his or her own way.

In like manner, God, the Father of this universe, takes great risk[17] when bearing the human race and does so because, more than anything else, He seeks to love and to be loved. He is, therefore, willing to create many and knows that some will turn their hearts toward Him, live a life of gratitude, and desire an intimate relationship with the Giver of all good gifts. The risk is high, but the reward immeasurable. Humans created in the image of God engage in the same activity. Genuine, authentic love is worth risking everything!

The Final Word

Like a roller-coaster ride the energy and passion around the table that night fluctuated up and down and all around. What began as a hopeful night of entertainment, and even belittlement, turned into perhaps the deepest conversation in which many of these people had ever engaged. There were those moments of serious introspection when each person was faced with life's ultimate questions, "What is my worth?" "For what am I living my life?" "Is the manner in which I use my freedom helping or destroying others?" Indeed, these are questions that could have been addressed long into the hours of the night. But the only foundation upon which such questions can be asked is a belief system that includes God. Only He can give authentic purpose. If we are nothing more than cosmic accidents, then the why question becomes illogical. This perfectly logical idea was beginning to be grasped by all those who attended the meeting. We had moved from "Does God exist?" to "Why does God do what He does?" As stated earlier, this is an entirely different question. Although we cannot possibly understand everything about God, there are many things about Him that have indeed been revealed if we will stop, think, and honestly pursue those answers. After three hours of conversation, we had now reached that point. Other than Dan, no one seemed angry with me. There was a sense that we were all on a journey together now, considering life's greatest questions and contemplating logical workable answers, we marched on into the night getting closer and closer to an end I never would have expected.

A Quick Application

Isn't it true that many parents, when they find their children heading down the wrong path, a path that leads to destruction, will begin to use various methods of deterrence to convince the child that he/she is going the wrong way and needs to change directions? When a son or daughter begins to use drugs or abuse alcohol or participate in indiscriminate sex, what parent sits idly by while the child continues down a destructive road?

In the same way, God refuses to sit on His hands while so much of the world places its value on temporary things. God's intention is to someday remove them because He does not want men and women whom He loves to depend upon such things for life's security.

I believe that God will do the same in your life. During those times when we begin to misplace our allegiance, desires, goals, and objectives towards those things that do not have the capacity to fulfill our lives, God will expose the insanity of such behavior by allowing us to see how fragile these things really are. He can do this in a number of ways.

He can strip material things from us, catalyzing the realization of how quickly fortune can fade. He can allow us, even energize us, to climb to the top of the corporate ladder so that we may experience the emptiness prestige can often bring. Or, He can use a physical illness to wake us up to the truth that, like the world and everything in it, we too are in decay and will one day fade away.

I believe God participates in such activity in order to move our thoughts toward eternal questions. He knows that we are focused upon the temporary to such a degree that eternity cannot easily be seen. Consequently, He reserves the right to open our eyes even through hardship and difficulty. Is it possible that God is presently working through the trials and hardships of your life to bring you to the questions of eternality? Perhaps He has orchestrated a few painful events in your life, specifically designed to spare you from a

---

greater, more serious tragedy. What parent would not do the same for the child he/she loves so much?

The next time difficulty comes, perhaps we should begin by asking, "God, what are you trying to tell me? Are you trying to save me from myself?"

Chapter Four

Why Does God Sit on His Hands?

*L*aura maintained her silence as Sherri chimed in again with a question that has longed plagued the greatest thinkers of our times. Actually, what she said seemed more like a statement rather than a question.

9:45 the table is opening . . .

Sherri's Second Issue

Sherri explained that one summer afternoon, she had been strolling downtown Brisbane on a summer afternoon, window-shopping and occasionally stopping for a coffee. As she sipped a cappuccino and participated in her favorite pastime (people watching), she witnessed a young man aggressively shove an elderly lady to the ground in order to snatch her purse. What Sherri remembered most was the fact that this whole endeavor did not happen quickly. Things got all tangled up and the robber, obviously not well experienced in elderly-lady-purse-snatching, panicked and became entangled in the purse strings. In Sherri's mind she had plenty of time to run over, kick the culprit, and rescue the old lady. Yet, not wanting to get involved, she just sat there and hoped the whole thing would just go away. The "oohs" and "ahs" around the table revealed disgust and surprise at Sherri's selfishness and apathy. Then Sherri dropped the bomb! She concluded, "If what I did was so wrong, then why does God sit idly by when others are being hurt when He has the power to do something about it? While I can accept that man is responsible for most of the pain and suffering in this world, and that where natural disasters are concerned, the earth may be revealing its decay, does this really nullify God's responsibility to limit the measure of destruction? You will have to admit, Jeff, God often seems to sit on His hands."

Did God set the universe in motion, grant freedom to each individual, then take an extended vacation not wanting to get involved in the day-to-day affairs of His handiwork? Does God not assume some responsibility to contain evil, to limit it? Or, does He let evil run rampant without restraint?

This Far and No Further

Any discussion about evil always includes a chapter detailing the events of the Holocaust. Hitler's Third Reich and the atrocities associated with it are some of the most horrific events known to man. To many, any possibility of God's existence dissipated when Hitler's S.S. men unleashed their hell upon the rest of the world, unhindered by any presupposed spiritual influence of morality, goodness, and justice.

Once again, it is crucial to point out that unless God exists, there are no absolute moral grounds upon which to judge the atrocities of the Third Reich as "evil." Without God, the reality of the Holocaust is nothing more than "survival of the fittest" and one group of chemicals disposing of another group of chemicals in what is truly the advancement of the superior elements. It is only in the context of God that we are able to ask our questions. We can, however, once again, attempt to harmonize the evil in the world with a good and perfect God who, at times, seems to sit on His hands.

Two people come to mind when this accusation against God surfaces. Both are noteworthy because they represent the thousands upon thousands whose stories will never be told.

Often associated with the Holocaust is Oscar Schindler, an industrialist whose entrepreneurial abilities far exceeded the top businessmen of his day. Schindler used all his bargaining skills to wheel and deal and save hundreds, if not thousands of Jews from the gas ovens, firing squads, and other atrocities associated with the death camps.

Opinions concerning Schindler's motivations vary. While some seem intent upon denouncing his efforts as anything but honorable and kind, and suggest instead that Schindler took advantage of the Jewish plight and found a convenient way to make a quick buck, the facts seem to suggest otherwise. In the end, Schindler lost everything and risked his very own life for the people he called, "his children." Today there are more than seven thousand descendants of his Jews living in the U.S., Europe, and Israel; seven thousand people who can trace their ancestry back to Schindler's factories. Is it any wonder that Oscar Schindler has become the object of everlasting gratitude by many in the Jewish community?

It is interesting to note that while Schindler's popularity has risen immensely over the past few years, thanks primarily to Steven Spielberg's Hollywood production and portrayal of his life, hundreds, if not thousands, of similar stories have since been told. One has to wonder if, while Hitler's regime was causing destruction, God worked behind the scenes in the human heart to rescue millions more from the death camps.

As I described Schindler's actions to Sherri, I posed a question, "Were the Oscar Schindler's of the world God's way of saying, "This far but no further?" Indeed, how many more would have died had God not intervened?

Sherri quickly chimed in, "Yes, Jeff, but six million died."

"Yes, but who is to blame—God or man?" I rebutted. "Did God pull the trigger? Did God fire up the gas ovens? Did God start World War II?"

"No, Jeff," Sherri demanded, "but He could have at least minimized the devastation."

"He did indeed minimize the damage," I said. "History has uncovered the fact that during Hitler's reign, God was indeed active, and used countless men and women who responded to the screams of the innocent and participated in an underground movement that ultimately limited the damage. The number of lives saved may not ever be known, but one thing is certain, God did not sit on His hands."

I went on to tell a second illustration. Another name that has become synonymous with victory over the Nazi death camps is Corrie Ten Boom. In her book, *The Hiding Place,* she describes how her father—a good and righteous, God-fearing man—with the assistance of a few carpenters built a secret room to save the lives of some of the Jews in their town. Though successful for a time, the Gestapo eventually arrested Corrie's father and sent Corrie and her sister, Betsie, to the death camps. Shifting from camp to camp, Corrie and Betsie ended up at Ravensbruck, a placed Corrie called, "hell on earth." They were beaten, starved, and forced to work long hours in the freezing cold. The fight to stay alive was never-ending.

In the midst of all this, Corrie and Betsie became emissaries of comfort and hope. Each evening before bedtime, the other women gathered around Corrie and Betsie to gain the emotional sustenance they needed to endure that pit of despair. The sisters would point them toward God, enunciating His hatred toward such atrocities while reminding them that, "No pit is too deep that God's love is not deeper still."[18]

As you read *The Hiding Place*, you cannot help but have your attention drawn to Corrie's trust and faith in God in the midst of the most horrific of circumstances. For example, Corrie and Betsie thanked God for the fleas that infested the Ravensbruck barracks at night. "Thank God for the fleas!" Betsie would say. Why? Because the fleas kept the guards away! This allowed the sisters to read the Bible to the inmates and point them to God whose love would sustain them and whose promise of something better catalyzed the type of hope that would not fail. Indeed, thank God for the fleas!

Man may be allowed to exact the evil of his free-will decisions but God is always working on the other side of the camp to give us what cannot be taken away—ultimate love and the promise of better things to come.

Admittedly, however, God does a bit more than all of that. Sometimes, He provides a special miracle. The following excerpt is from a condensed version of Corrie's story.

> *Once again it was roll-call. The women stamped their feet to keep warm. Suddenly Corrie heard her name: "Prisoner ten Boom, report after roll-call."*
>
> *What was going to happen? Was she going to be punished? Or shot?*
>
> *"Father in heaven, please help me now," she prayed.*
>
> *When she reported, she was given a card stamped "Entlassen," which means "Released." She was free! She could hardly believe it. She was given back her few possessions, some new clothes and a railway pass back to Holland. After a long, hard journey, she arrived back among friends in her own country. Afterwards she learned that she had been released by mistake!*[19]

By mistake? Or did God intervene? Did He say, "This far and no further?" Our finite minds struggle with this proposition. Although story after story suggests divine intervention, we have great difficulty in believing that God was responsible for such a mistake. Instead, we want God to send fire down on the Ravensbruck guards, singeing everything in sight except, of course, the prisoners. A God who works behind the scenes does not appeal to us. Yet, if we would but stop and consider the free-will mechanism given to every man, we would begin to understand why God works the way He does.

Ironically, if God did rain fire down upon Hitler's regime, no doubt there would be many who would say, "How can a loving, good God do such a thing?" This is similar to the response the Christians receive when someone screams in their faces, "Why does your God sit on His hands in the midst of all this evil?" and the Christians respond, "He does not sit on His hands. He is taking notes! One day everyone will give an account for the manner in which he uses his freedom. One day justice will roll like a river." To which the accuser replies, "How could a good God of love punish people?"

In today's world, God cannot win. Whether He acts or refuses to act, the world is never void of protestors accusing God of injustice. *The truth is we have made God in our own image.* Rather than asking, "What is God like?" We continue to tell Him what He should be without understanding the myriad of contradictions. We want justice without punishment, prevention without intervention, and relationship without sacrifice. These are logical impossibilities, which a logical God refuses to violate.

Perhaps in the most aggressive tone of the evening, I reminded Sherri that there are many events in life that have no other explanation other than the hand of God. Unfortunately, when He intervenes, we have great difficulty admitting and embracing His activity.

Seeing the Unseen

When I was a little boy, a traveling circus came to town that featured the largest roller coaster I had ever seen! (I hadn't gotten out much.) All the boys and girls in my hometown ran to stand in line to experience the rush and thrill of being thrown around in an old iron car. I will never forget Tommy Crowe. I was never good with names, but for some reason everyone who grew up in the little town of Elizabethton, Tennessee, knows that name. He was the little boy who fell out of the roller coaster and died. I sat on my mother's knee and contemplated Tommy's death. I thought to myself, *Why did God not protect little Tommy?* On Sundays we would drive by Tommy's house on the way home from church, and our hearts would sink to think of the pain in the heart of a mother who had lost her little boy. "Why?" I would ask myself. "Why could God not have prevented such a tragedy?" Over the years I have come to recognize two immutable truths in relation to this question.

First, God can and does prevent such tragedies every single day of our lives. Second, even when God does not intervene to prevent the tragedy, He is still working behind the scenes to say, "This far no further!" My Grandmother Bessie used to pray for me every day. As my brothers and I would walk home from school, she would always pray that our journey be a safe one. When Tommy died, I asked my mother if perhaps Tommy's grandmother failed to pray for him. Her response was classic. She reminded me that in our humanity we can only see and understand the things that are visible. We must consider the times that God plants the thought in the life of a child to take the shortcut through the field or stop by some other place on the way home, or stay at school just five minutes more before walking home, all for the purpose of diverting the child's path away from a drunk driver, or a pedophile, or some other unfortunate event.

The problem with us is that we cannot see the unseen. Moreover, we tend to focus on life's occasional destructive events, rather than the goodness that abounds in our own lives every day.

A great example of this human tendency was illustrated during Larry King's interview with Billy Graham. King asked, "What are we to make of these television preachers who preach of morality and then fail so miserably to live up to their own standards?" The question was asked in the context of the demise of Jim Bakker. Graham, who seldom enters into any conversation that might shed a negative light on anyone, yielded a thought-provoking response. He reminded Larry King of all the airplanes that take off and land every day. Thousands upon thousands of aircraft in hundreds and hundreds of places, all taking off and landing safely without one word of praise or mention in the press. Yet, when one plane experiences difficulty, it is front page news on every newsstand across the globe.

Similarly, thousands and thousands of Christian lives have been changed for good. Thousands upon thousands persistently resist temptation, patiently overcome trials, and passionately pursue lives of purity. In any given day, millions of attempts to live such lives are successful. Yet, there is no mention of their lives. But when one proclaimed Christian fails, then the response is: Let's throw the rest of them out. They are all hypocrites. What if we did the same to airplanes?

God does not sit on His hands. Because of man's rejection and refusal to connect with the Creator and live a life of gratitude, evil runs rampant in our world. However, *for every evil event that occurs there are dozens of good events that happen.* God says, "This far and no further," as He combats evil with a plan of His own. We will never know the reason for little Tommy's death. What is certain, however, is that for every life taken by unfortunate and evil circumstances (the roller coaster was later shown to be poorly maintained) another life is spared by God's unseen hand.

Knowing why God spares some while allowing others to die is something that will never be known. Again, we are finite and He is infinite. This does not nullify the fact, however, that

Why Does God Sit on His Hands?

God does intervene even in the midst of man's free-will decisions. Perhaps we think He should intervene more. Perhaps we think He should save more lives. But before we run around screaming, "Why, God?" remember, He is looking down from heaven, passionately pleading with free-will men and women, asking "Why, Man? Why do you use your freedom to hurt one another? Why do you insist upon living for your own selfish agenda and self-aggrandizement? Why do you not love your neighbor as yourself?"

Quick Application

Have you ever wondered what God's plan is for your life? I mean, if there is a God, it seems logical to assume He would have a plan and a purpose for creating you. In fact, in a world that features a sovereign Creator, every event you experience would have an ultimate purpose.

Furthermore, whatever calling God has placed upon your life, whatever grand task He has made you to do, He would assume the responsibility to equip you to do it. Creating you for some grand purpose without equipping you to do it makes little sense! According to David, one of the greatest warriors and conquerors who ever lived, such equipping begins in your mother's womb and continues to evolve until you are ready to play the part for which you were born. He wrote,

> For You created my inmost being;
>   You knit me together in my mother's womb.
> I praise You because I am fearfully and wonderfully made;
>   your works are wonderful,
>   I know that full well.
> My frame was not hidden from you
>   when I was made in the secret place.
> When I was woven together in the depths of the earth,
>   your eyes saw my unformed body.
> All the days ordained for me
>   were written in your book
>   before one of them came to be. (Psalm 139:13-16)

True, many will refuse to ask the question of purpose. They will continue to live for themselves and to stockpile material things until death do they part. Even so, God will continue to orchestrate and fashion together events in every life to train and equip each one to accomplish the purpose for which they have been born.

Here is the point. What God allows in your life and what He keeps out is all part of the equipping. Choosing the purpose for which we will use our talents and abilities is a special privilege, and even if we choose to live for our own self-aggrandizement, the equipping will never cease so that, when the day comes in which we turn to God, we will be "armed and ready" to accomplish the very purpose for which we have been made. Often, people who have endured the most hardship are the very ones who have made the greatest impact on the world. It appears that the more trouble God allows to come into your life, the greater your potential to change the world.

So, the next time you find yourself in difficult waters, ask yourself, "Is all of this part of my preparation to be used by God for a grand purpose?" Approaching your life with this attitude is a crucial step toward finding your significance and living the abundant life you so desperately seek.

Chapter Five

What in the World Is God Doing?

*W*hen it comes to pain and suffering, much of what we experience in this world is the result of free-will creatures using their freedom in an abusive manner. Asking why God does not step in more often and prevent much of the pain is a fair question. However, again, the question itself needs to be examined. Implying that God should do more to stifle evil in this world is to imply that "evil" as a moral category exists. As we discussed in chapter one, this is impossible without an absolute moral lawgiver, God.

Second, the question assumes that God does not intervene very often, when in reality, there is no way to know how often He does raise His hand and say, "This far, no further." Our knowledge is limited and finite. There is no possible way we would or could have the faintest idea of the ratio between God's intervention and His decision to allow events to continue without interference. This is especially valid when we consider God's ability to work everything together to accomplish His purposes. We will discuss this issue in more detail below.

Finally, as we have shown in the previous chapter, history is filled with examples where God seemed to intervene in an impressive fashion.

Sherri seemed content for the moment with my response. Again, serious introspection permeated the room, in what seemed to be a moment for each to consider the times God had indeed spared them from a greater tragedy. "There but for the grace of God go I" has become a popular theme in our subjective, postmodern world, once again unveiling the contradictions. But this is where our story moves to another level of intensity. I took a sip of Diet Coke and glanced down toward the end of the table where Laura was seated. I noticed that all was not well with the management. Laura seemed visibly disturbed, and from experience I knew that the volcano was about to erupt! Then suddenly, instead of anger, sadness overwhelmed her as the tears began to flow. The truth of the matter was about to come out.

10:30 P.M. and all is not well . . .

Although Laura's staff respected her, very little relationship, other than superficial pleasantries, existed between them. Her business acumen and sharp-dressed presentation impressed, but also intimidated, each of them.

Expecting Laura's employees to come to her aid, I waited patiently for someone to move to her side and find out what was the matter. Instead, like a pride of lions afraid to approach the male, each cub cowered away from the scene and refocused their attention toward me. This turn of events took us down a path of no return.

As Laura shed tears and Sherri demanded more explanation concerning God's involvement in the midst of evil circumstances, I decided it was time to cut to the chase and take our table to a place they had all been before. I calmly asked for and received permission from Sherri and Jucinda for a bit of freedom to explore this issue further. Then I related the following true events that had personally changed my life and allowed me to see the bigger picture of a God who not only refused to sit on His hands but, from the very beginning, had a plan to combat the evil in this world while respecting the free will of every creature.

But first let me recount one of the most captivating stories I have ever heard as told by Ravi Zacharias in one of his classic sermons. He spoke of a woman named Edith Taylor from Walter, Massachusetts. Edith had found the love for which she had been searching and was anticipating growing old with a man to whom she was more than willing to give her heart. After the marriage, things began to go as planned until her husband was called away to serve his country in the military. Separated by a great distance, letters of love and appreciation frequently passed between them. The children desperately missed their father, and Edith longed to be reunited with the man she loved. As she waited unwearyingly for the family to be made whole again, Edith sent letters reminding her husband of her unfailing love and devotion. Unfortunately, one day, correspondence from her husband stopped coming. At first Edith feared the worst—perhaps something drastic had occurred; maybe her husband had been killed or captured. One can only imagine the devastation Edith must have felt when she discovered the truth about her husband's silence. One morning, she found a letter in the post that broke her heart. As Ravi retold the story, I remember him quoting something like this:

> Edith, there is no easy way to say what I am about to say. I know your heart will be broken, but, I am writing to tell you that I have met a young Japanese woman and will not be returning home after the war. I am going to remain here in Japan and begin a new life, and start a new family.

Devastated, Edith's hopes and dreams were shattered. For a time, Edith withheld the news from her young sons. The thought of shedding a bad light on their father was simply too much for her to endure. Soon, however, her twelve-year-old son began to ask questions: "Mommy, why doesn't Daddy write to us anymore? Does he not love us anymore?" Edith thought that perhaps it was time for the truth, so she told the little boy: "No, I guess Daddy doesn't love us anymore. He has a new wife and a new family."

Her son's response could not have been anticipated. "Mommy, just because Daddy doesn't love us, does that mean we can't love him? Can't we still write to Daddy and tell him how we are doing and ask him how he is doing?" Enduring a broken heart Edith responded, "Well, yes, I suppose that we can do that." So, the letters and photographs continued back and forth for the years to come. Each time Edith opened a new letter or viewed new photos of a new family, her wounds would reopen. Then one day, in a cruel twist, Edith received a letter from her husband. Words could never express how she felt as she discovered a strange, if not cruel request. He had been diagnosed with cancer and was not expected to live more than a few months. Having made no provisions for his new family, and holding very little money, he begged Edith to take his new wife and children into her home and teach them to stand on their own two feet. According to the story, this is exactly what happened. Edith's unfaithful husband put his lover and their children on a plane to the United States, and Edith raised the children of a betrayed love, teaching them to stand on their own feet and giving them a fighting chance in this world.

Truly this is an uncommon story, featuring an uncommon woman. The question is: What could make a woman so willing to do such a thing? How could she muster up the courage, forgiveness, grace, and mercy required to do what she did? Edith was in no way wealthy. The coming years of giving assistance to a woman who in no way deserved her mercy, coupled with children who would demand great sacrifices, would exhaust her energy and finance. Yet, willingly, graciously, and joyfully, she did what needed to be done. I find her explanation compelling:

> In that dark, dreary, hellish situation, I thank God for the ray of light and hope to share some of the love of God in this very dismal setting.[20]

Yes, everything about Edith's situation was dark and dreary. **If love is the highest "good" in this universe, then surely, betrayed love is the greatest "evil."** The popular saying that "No one can hurt us like the ones we love," rings true time and time again. The deeper we give ourselves to someone, the deeper the pain when betrayal occurs. For this reason alone, many choose not to love. For them, the risk is too great. Edith stands in stark contrast to the manner in which most people respond to betrayal. Why? Because she knew she experienced the love of God when she least deserved it. So, she decided to bring that same unconditional love into an evil situation in the hopes that she could take something that was bad and turn it around for good. Only a person who lives life for something greater than themselves could ever accomplish such a feat. Edith's story is our first clue to God's plan to combat evil in our world.

Common Love

I saw the traits of Edith Taylor modeled regularly in the life of my mother. She, my mother, was a tremendous woman whose life was cut tragically short. As I sit here in Whangarei, New Zealand, getting ready to write the following words, I know the task will not be easy. Having lost my mother not too long ago, the wounds have not healed, and the ongoing conversation with God as to why He would allow such a thing is not over. She was only sixty-one years young. A picture of health, her beautiful blue eyes and lovely blond hair (which she insisted upon dying strawberry blonde) was only outdone by her slim and trim figure, the envy of every woman. Although I have not spent very much time in the United States, I have always drawn a sense of strength from knowing my mother would always be there when I needed her. Yearly visits were a great highlight of my life.

A lady who oozed with goodness, my mother had overcome a childhood that featured little love and plenty of condemnation. Yet, she managed to break the cycle. She was not perfect, but neither was I the perfect child. In fact, my three brothers and I surely drove her to the line of insanity many times. Yet she always seemed to recover quickly and maintain her love for both us and God. And I loved her back.

On a warm summer day at about three o'clock in the afternoon, I received a call on my cell phone. Seeing the prefix 011 on the front of the call told me that the call originated from the United States. My youngest brother was on the line. He said, "Jeff, I have some bad news. Mom is in the hospital, I do not think she is going to make it." I said, "What!? What do you mean Mom is not going to make it?! She is a picture of health! What's going on?" My brother went on to describe how my mother was sitting on the edge of the bed speaking with our grandmother, when suddenly she fainted and collapsed to the floor. The paramedics were there in only four minutes, but, it was too late. My mother had passed away due to a cardiac myopathy. Different from a heart attack, my mother would have felt no pain. Her heart simply slowed down until it stopped beating. The process probably took about twenty minutes. She would not have known anything was wrong, but would have simply passed out due to lack of oxygen. My brother told me that they rushed her to the hospital and placed her on a ventilator.

I drove my car as fast as I could to the airport. I was alone in the car and then on the airplane for more than twenty hours. During this time, my battle with God began.

"How could You do this?!" I demanded. "This was a fine woman who was an asset to the community. She praised and worshiped You wherever she went. Not a day went by that she did not talk to some troubled teenager about You and Your goodness and mercy and grace. For forty-five years she never failed to remind people of Your passion to enter into a relationship whereby You would guide, lead, and empower them as they live the journey of life. Surely, that is worth something! Is it too much to ask that You prolong her life a bit? I mean, would it have been that difficult for You who made the earth and the seas to spare the life of such a beautiful, God-fearing person?"

No matter how hard I tried to fight it, these questions and accusations surfaced again and again. During the entire trip back to the States I wrestled with God and these issues. When I entered the hospital room where my mother lay lifeless, I knew that the end was near. Only able to breath with the assistance of man's machines, her chest moved up and down as oxygen was forced into her lungs. I knelt down beside the bed and prayed the hardest and most intense prayer of my life. "Lord," I said, "I know You have the power to raise my mother out of that hospital bed and bring her back to life. I know You can make it as though none of this ever happened. Please, Lord, please, would You do it?"

I had read somewhere that people in comas can often hear the things happening around them. So I decided to be bold and whisper in my mother's ear. I told her that I loved her and could not live without her. I kept saying to her, "Wake up! Please wake up! I love you. I love you. Please don't leave me."

I do not know how to describe what happened next. All I can tell you is that a tear rolled down her cheek and her heart rate began to beat at a faster rate. I thought I was bringing her back, so I increased the volume of my whispers almost to a shout. "Please, Mommy, please come back! I am nothing without you. I need you. Please don't leave me. Come back. Come back!"

She did not come back.

Hours later the nurses ran into the waiting room and told us that our mother's heart was fibrillating again and this would probably signify the end. We rushed into the room, witnessed a woman in pain and decided, as a family, that it was time to let her go.

The moment they took my mother off the ventilator was undeniably the worst event of my life. Taking one last breath, she was gone. As I stood beside her hospital bed, I felt weaker than ever before. Deeply moved, I wept uncontrollably. My brothers and their families went back to the family home, tired, frustrated, and unsure how each would cope with this loss. Our greatest concern was for our father. He loved our mother as much as any man could. For forty-plus years he had been undeniably faithful and unwaveringly devoted to Mom. Not being one to openly express his feelings, we feared that Dad would bottle all the hurt and pain until one day it would finally kill him. The days until the funeral were restless. My inquisition concerning God intensified, and I demanded answers. I never received a bolt of lightning nor a trance-type vision, but the answers did come. As I write this, some seven years after her death, the clarity with which my questions have been answered is astounding.

Although God did not reveal everything immediately, He didn't wait very long to begin confronting me with my own presuppositions. The day after the funeral my father and I were sitting on the front-porch swing, reflecting on all that had happened. In his own gentle way, Dad looked at me, smiled, and said, "You know, Jeff, I just can't figure out why God took your mother from me so soon." It was that word "took" that disturbed me. As if God simply looked down to earth and said, "OK, send the death angel down to collect Betty Vines. Her time is up."

Immediately I fired back at my father, "Dad, God did not 'take' our mother from us. You heard the doctor; Mom's heart stopped beating. She possessed a genetic defect. This flesh is not eternal. Each of us has our own things with which we deal: poor diet; the hole in the ozone; the fertilizers we use;

the stress we allow to dominate our lives; the overdoses of caffeine; or a myriad of other things found in an imperfect world. Any one of them could have been the culprit."

Not missing a beat Dad replied, "Yes, Son, but God could have easily prevented Betty's death."

"Yes, Dad, but that is different to suggesting that God *took* my mother away," I responded. "No doubt He could have prevented her death, but that does not mean that He took her away in some executive, arbitrary decision. On one hand I think God is just as sad as we are. He feels the pain of our loss, but for reasons beyond us, He chose to allow this event to occur."

This statement provoked an interesting response from my father. "Jeff," he asked, "could you please tell me for what reason God would allow your mother to pass away when there was so much good yet to be done by a life so well lived?"

Knowing my father's faith was not in jeopardy but that he was merely looking for answers, I made a commitment to him. "In time," I promised, "both of us will know, and we will embrace God just as Mom said that we always should."

Again, my conversation with Dad took place some time ago. Here we are, years later, and I can honestly say that although the pain never goes away, clarity has come. And these are only the reasons of which I am aware. Only God has an exhaustive understanding of the painful events of our lives.

My mother's prayer-life consisted of four major daily requests. First, her deepest desire was that her four sons would love, assist, and encourage one another through life. Her passion for this went way beyond the typical maternal desire to see her family unified. Mom came from a broken, seriously dysfunctional family, and was determined to break this cycle and raise a family that longed for each others' company. I watched as through the years my mother—no matter how tired or fatigued—prepared banquets for her children to enjoy. The last few years before her death I would see her work a hard week at the local supermarket and then arrive home on Christmas Eve to spend the next twenty-four hours in the kitchen preparing a meal fit for a king (and all his subjects). Having her children together in harmony on Christmas Eve meant more to Mom than all the Mother's Day, birthday, and Christmas gifts combined. Apart from her faith in God, she treasured Christmas dinner above all other events.

Unfortunately, as the years passed my brothers and I began to grow apart. Everything imaginable began to drive a wedge between us: political, social, parental, and even religious differences turned what used to be peaceful times around the table into verbal fiascos. Hatred never existed between my brothers and me, but the closeness once enjoyed began to quickly fade. This broke my mother's heart. The more we grew apart, the harder she tried to restore and repair the damage. Late one evening while I was sitting on the sofa with my mom, she began to cry. When I asked her what was the matter, she replied, "I just want you boys to love one another." I assured her that we did, but in my heart I knew that the love had become superficial, at best. I also realized at that point that we were all to blame: pride, arrogance, and the need to be right had tarnished what used to be pure and sacred. Every night after reading her Bible my mother would pray, "Please, God, do whatever You need to do to bring my children together." This is a mother's prayer of desperation. Make no mistake; my mother knew the magnitude of such prayer. She used to warn me with the popular axiom, "Be careful what you ask for; you may get it!"

Secondly, my mother prayed especially for me. This is not to say that she did not pray for my other brothers as well. I am sure she had similar conversations with them. I am not aware of all that passed between Mom and the others. I am aware, however, of my mother confronting me on my thirtieth birthday with an uncharacteristic tone. In her mind, as I became more widely known, I was "getting too big for my britches." My writing and speaking did not seem to impress her as much as I thought it should. Don't misunderstand. She was proud of me, but was concerned. During my birthday celebration she gave me a stern warning. She said, "Jeff, I am concerned about you."

"Why on earth would you be concerned about me?" I asked. She quickly chimed in, "Because even though you have a sharp intellect, your passion for people is lacking." Feeling this was unfair I sharply rebuked her and said, "How do you know that? On what do you base your comments? I love people!" Unnerved by the never-ending examples with which she had come prepared, I began to realize that she was right! I was devastated. In my immaturity I had become more concerned about winning an argument than lovingly helping the other person. Seeing my hurt, Mom placed her arm around me and said, "Son, I only tell you this because I love you, and I know that you will accomplish great things, but you must get this one thing right." Then she quoted Charles Swindoll's famous line, "People will not care how much you know until they know how much you care." Every night, Mom would pray for me, fearful that this one thing lacking in my life would stifle my greatest potential.

Third, my mother prayed diligently that God would not allow the death of my father to precede her own. I am not sure my brothers and I will ever fully comprehend this. In my mind it was a foolish prayer, especially when you consider that our father's life expectancy was about fifty years. He came from a long line of heart-attack prone people. Being the youngest in the family, one by one he watched as his older brothers passed away, all from sudden heart attacks. I think Mom knew this and begged God to protect our father and to allow her to go on to heaven before Dad. Part of the reason for this strange request is that no man loved his wife like our father. Mother came from a home with unstable relationships. Her father was not loved and consequently found it difficult to express appreciation, gratitude, and love for anything or for anyone. Mom had prayed for a God-fearing man when she was younger, one that would love and cherish her, and she got him! Not wanting to return to the life she previously endured, she could not imagine life without Dad. So, she prayed.

Finally, and the one most difficult to record, my mother regularly prayed a special prayer for my brother Tony. Blessed with most of the talent in the family, today, he is the most successful of the Vines boys. Successful, but not in the way we tend to measure success. When I say 'successful,' I mean doing what one does best to the highest degree.[21]

As successful as Tony is today, no one can possibly understand what he went through as a child. He was overweight, physically unattractive, and he bore the brunt of many jokes. He did not have the same build as the other Vines boys and was often not included in various activities. Sadly, most of his young life was a life of rejection. What made it worse was the fact that in Mom's mind, whether she would admit it or not, Tony reminded her of her own childhood; a time that she desperately wanted to forget.

Mom endured a rough beginning; she was so skinny that names like beanpole, string bean, and Gumby were commonplace in the schoolyard. These were days that Mom never wanted to think about again. Yet when Tony came along, she was forced to relive her past, and it was too much for her. Unconsciously, she treated Tony differently from the rest of us. Ironic, isn't it? The thing we need most from others is the very thing we are so unwilling to give. No parent is perfect, and although Mom was a great Mom, she had her flaws just like everybody else.

In the midst of rejection from the outside world Tony needed to come home and find acceptance. Instead, he was often ridiculed at home as well for nothing more than being physically what he was at that time: overweight and seemingly unattractive.

Mother's realization that she had treated Tony differently from the others absolutely devastated her in later years. Counseling bandaged the wounds but did not erase the pain; it merely helped her acknowledge and begin to deal with it. During the last ten years of her life she prayed daily for forgiveness and would consistently ask Tony for it. There was a part of Tony that wanted to give it, but there was another part that wanted to make her pay for what she had done. Forgiveness for Tony was a day-to-day thing. Some days, he would give forgiveness liberally; other days, especially if Mom made him angry, forgiveness would not be forthcoming. Mom knew this and prayed desperately for the relationship between her and Tony to be fully restored. She knew that only God could do this.

Answered Prayers

When my mother died, the heartbreak my brothers and I experienced was unbearable. My greatest regret to this day is that I did not get a chance to say goodbye. Had I known she was going away, I would have told her how much I really loved her and how much I needed and valued her as a mom. I can never have that chance again. And so I say, before I continue on, if your mother is still living, go to her and tell her that you love her; forget about all her failures, she is only human. Perhaps if you would have been a more perfect child, she would have been a more perfect mother. Imperfection breeds imperfection. This is an imperfect world where each of us carries our flaws into every relationship. It is a vicious cycle that will never be totally cured. We can only hope to improve with every coming year in hopes of not passing the damage done to us on to the next generation. So embrace your mother. She did the best she could with what she had. If forgiveness is required, forgive her. But love her and tell her that you love her. The healing that will take place in your own life is worth every ounce of effort you can muster. Tell her you love her, or you will regret your silence for the rest of your life.

When my mother passed away, a chain reaction was set in motion that, to this day, can be clearly seen. First, my brothers and I became inseparable. We got involved in each other's lives. We frequently ask about each other's children and possess a genuine concern and goodwill for one another. My dad feared that Mom's death would drive us farther apart. Indeed, Mom was the glue that held us together. But her death seemed to have a catalytic effect. I guess we all began to realize how petty our differences were and that, all in all, Mom had done a tremendous job of raising us and needed to be honored in a very special way.

However, answered prayer doesn't stop there. Something drastic happened to me when my mother died. It is almost as if my entire personality experienced an overhaul! As you have probably guessed by now, I am a "momma's boy." That's right! I admit it, and am very proud of it. Recognizing the sacrifices our mother made for us, I never held back the praise. While I was in university playing basketball and traipsing all over the country, my mother was working to provide the extra money required for the additional expenses not covered by my scholarship. Understanding her sacrifice I sat down in the dormitory one afternoon and wrote her a letter. My father told me that when Mom read the letter, she cried for an hour. The point is that I was very close to Mom and developed an appreciation for her at a very young age. When things went wrong, I ran to her arms. I felt that I had a home there. As long as Mom was around, I felt safe and secure. Facing the world did not seem that big of a deal. This is a feeling that I took with me right on into marriage and into my twenties and thirties. Please do not misunderstand. Mother always pointed me toward God. She knew that He could work wonders and grant me a peace that passed understanding; she wanted me to run to Him. I was fully aware of this. Just knowing that she would give such good advice comforted and sustained me through difficult times in both Africa and New Zealand.

When she died, my whole world was shaken. But something else—something never anticipated—happened as well. All of a sudden I began to notice the pain of others around me. Others who had lost a father, mother, son, or daughter seemed to matter much more to me now. Experiencing the loss of my mother and the depth and intensity of the pain associated with such loss made me realize that I am not alone in this world. Others are hurting and struggling to the same degree. When I returned to New Zealand after the funeral, I was supposed to speak at a service held at Massey University. I was scheduled to begin a four-part series entitled: Creation vs. Evolution. Instead, with the audience fully aware of what I had just been through, I scrapped my notes and shot from the hip. Opening my heart, feeling deeply for those in a similar situation, I spoke as I had never spoken before. The head was still present, but the heart overflowed and changed the tone and emotion of my message. It was a change that would go with me from that day forward. Instead of merely delivering the facts, I looked into the eyes of the audience and realized that my questions were their questions and that we all were in this thing together. In my mind it was then that our weekly broadcast on PRIME television really took off! Our audience doubled, if not tripled, in numbers and a connection between the viewer and me developed that still exists to this day. My messages had not changed that much, but the manner in which I delivered them changed dramatically.

When I was twenty-two years old, I delivered what I believed to be an exhaustive and fail-proof address on the topic of pain and suffering. Yet, the audience seemed unmoved. My father-in-law, who is a great speaker in his own right, told me that the reason the response did not match the material was simple: "You cannot speak about that which you yourself have not experienced." Most twenty-two-year-olds have not endured enough pain to even superficially understand the hurts and emotions of the masses. After my mother's death, however, the facts of pain and suffering came to life, and every address on the issue was a life-breathing dissertation that impacted those who lived in the real world. These were not merely abstract ideas but heartfelt realities. When Mom died, I never knew that a person could hurt so much and still be alive. That changed my perspective. My mother's prayer was answered. People matter to me; it's more than just having the right answers to difficult questions. It's all about loving and being genuinely concerned for others with no strings attached.

As I acknowledge the obvious answer to my mother's prayer concerning my father, I now move on to the final piece of the puzzle. I experienced a deep movement in my spirit as I witnessed Mother's last breath, and weeping as I had never wept before, I stood up with a resolve to gather my emotions and help my brothers through this ordeal. My father needed help now; plans for a funeral had to be made: family members had to be contacted, and a minister's services would need to be requested. I glanced around the room plotting my next move when I noticed that someone was missing from the hospital room, my brother Tony. Genuinely concerned, I began frantically searching the hospital. Tony was nowhere to be found. I thought he might have slipped out for a smoke, so I checked the four corners of the outside building, to no avail. Finally, I shifted my search indoors and began looking throughout every corridor until I discovered Tony curled up in the fetal position, crying out for his mother. When I saw him,

I felt great pity. "Oh Tony," I said, "what's wrong?" His reply? "My mommy is dead, Jeff. My mommy is dead."

Days after the funeral, Tony and I talked about his relationship to Mom. He told me about how he had been reaching out to her in his own quiet way, and how he believed they were making some progress. Then, as we both found it difficult to sleep one morning, we made our way down to the local greasy spoon, ordered some coffee, and chatted until the sun came up. With the promise of a new day so gloriously expressed in an east Tennessee sunrise came the realization that Tony had now totally and completely forgiven his mother and cherished her in a manner that none of us could possibly comprehend.

He collected pictures of Mom ranging from her childhood on into her formative years and pasted them on a poster as a tribute to her life. He found a photograph of Mom that portrayed the blond-haired, blue-eyed beauty into which she evolved by the time she was twenty-two. Most remarkable, however, was the song he wrote on her behalf.

What Mother was unable to accomplish in life, she did in death. I wonder now if perhaps her greatest prayer was that the damage she had done to Tony might somehow be forgiven and healed. Although she sensed God's forgiveness, she desperately wanted Tony's. When Mom died, Tony's perspective totally changed. Again, my mother's prayer was answered in full!

Sherri's Objection

As I related the events of my mother's death, you could hear the frustration in Sherri's voice when she loudly demanded, "Are you suggesting that God took the life of your mother in order to answer her prayers?" Without hesitation I responded, "Absolutely not. Instead I suggested that because God knows all things, He is fully aware of the number of our days. He knows precisely when and where the end will come for each of us. Death is not optional. It comes to all. However, God doesn't just look down one day and say, "OK, Pal, your time is up!" No, the timing of our death is a result of various factors, such as, diet, exercise, climate, pollution, stress, natural calamities, and, perhaps most of all, genetic weaknesses passed from generation to generation. My mother died at age sixty-one not because God zapped her but because of an imperfect body in an imperfect world that has been severely tarnished by the effects of free-will decisions for thousands of years.

The point, however, is that God *is never caught off guard.* He knows precisely the ramifications that evil has exacted upon our lives, and He is poised ready to combat evil with good. There is a verse in the Bible that must be quoted here: "And we know that in all things God works for the good of those who love him, who have been called according to his purpose" (Romans 8:28.)

The Point

God does not sit idly by and allow evil to run rampant. God takes what is often the result of evil and uses it for some eternal good. From the fleas of a concentration camp to the death of a loved and cherished mother, and even in the midst of betrayed love, God is always working things together for good.

A Quick Application

Hours ago, when the evening began, everyone in the room assumed that God had not been active in combating evil. As the hours passed, however, a feeling that God combats every action of evil with an action of good began permeating the room.

I know of no greater example of this than in the Old Testament character Joseph. (Read Genesis 37 and 39–45.) Joseph experienced hardship after hardship. Indeed, it would be safe to assume that Joseph probably felt as if he were the target of some evil, sinister plan. Every time Joseph made a morally good decision, it was

---

met with evil consequences. Barely keeping his head above water Joseph continued to do the right thing. What looked like a road of evil and destruction became a road of victory in which one man was able to save an entire nation from literal extinction.

Joseph's story proved to be the ultimate illustration to solidify my supposition that God does not sit on His hands and is always working in our lives to accomplish His purposes. Indeed, sometimes His purposes allow us to go through painful times, but He uses those times to mold and shape and squeeze us until the good stuff comes out. The manner in which we respond to the trials of our lives will greatly depend upon that for which we live our lives. So, may I ask you? For what grand purpose are you living your life?

If we are incredibly selfish and believe that the world owes us an easy convenient life, then we will fight, kick, and scream when trouble comes our way. However, if we live our lives for a purpose greater than ourselves, understanding that the world, while thoroughly enjoyable, is riddled with the ramifications of man's free-will decisions, then we will look to the One who will take a disadvantage, turn it into an advantage, and use it for ultimate good.

Chapter Six

Can God Recover?

11 P.M. and time is running out . . .

OK, Jeff, I can see your point in all of this," muttered Jucinda. "I will admit that there have been times I have experienced pain in my life, only to see such suffering result into some great good I never imagined possible (*I sensed a "but" coming on*), but (*told you*) what possible good came to the children trapped under the waters of a tsunami? While God is achieving His purpose of allowing the earth to reveal its futility, little children who have not had the chance to experience life are being snuffed out, (snapping her fingers) just like that! *What possible good comes to those children?"*

When Jucinda brought up the tsunami issue again, I remembered how the day after the Asian Tsunami struck, a large percentage of the media stories and photographs focused upon the little children. In Jucinda's mind God could not possibly recover from allowing those little children to be swept away in a moment of great fear and terror.

The dialogue which occurred between Jucinda and me was a climactic point in the evening. Our conversation served as the bridge into, what most around the table would have considered, unfamiliar territory. In a way, Jucinda opened the door to a beautiful topic and in doing so, anyone in the room who had begun leaning toward an early departure, now firmly planted himself into his chair, contemplating deeply the words that would follow. In order to fully grasp what happened I have written the dialogue down in an orderly fashion. While neither her nor my words are exact, they are extremely close, and in no way lose the punch of the specific conclusion.

Jeff: In response to your comment that God could not possibly recover from allowing the children of the tsunami to suffer and die before they had lived a full life, I would like to ask you a few questions.

Jucinda: By all means, please.

Jeff: You stated earlier that life here on earth—with all its challenges, fears, tragedies, and atrocities—is an unpleasant life, correct?

Jucinda: Absolutely. There is so much in this world that is not good!

Jeff: If that is the case, would God not seem kind to prevent a child from growing up and having to experience the frustrations and fears associated with living in this world? Allowing the child to be swept up and out of this life before the heartache of adulthood begins would be an act of mercy, would it not?

Jucinda: No, no, no. That is not what I meant. Even though there is so much wrong with this world, there is still so much about life that is enjoyable: relationships, love, the ocean, recreation, all of these make life interesting and livable.

Jeff: I firmly agree. I just wanted you to recognize again that while God allows evil to exist for the moment, He has provided so much good in this world that life can be thoroughly enjoyed in the midst of even the most unpleasant situations. For instance, the love of my wife during the loss of my mother proved to be an enjoyable sustaining treasure for which I will always be grateful.[22]

Jucinda: OK, so life has plenty of good to go along with the bad. What is your point?

Jeff: My point is that it is God who gave life to that child who died in the tsunami. If He gave life once, He can give it again. From our human perspective, the child is gone forever and has missed out of all the joy associated with life here on earth. However, from God's perspective, as soon as that child was covered with the tsunami waters, his/her next waking moment saw the hand of God reach down and pull him/her up towards heaven to a place where there is no pain, suffering, hunger or death. In fact, Jucinda, I don't think that this child feels he has been cheated. He has no desire to return. What he has now is what we all long for: perfect, unhindered relationship between Creator and creature in a place where the Giver of all good gifts showers indescribable blessings upon those whom He loves.

Jucinda: But, Jeff, a lot of people have to endure horrible, tragic lives before they ever get to a place like that. I am assuming you are talking about heaven, a place which I happen to believe in, but what about the Nazi death camps? What about a life of sexual abuse? What about people who are the victims of horrendous crimes? What about the severely handicapped? The list goes on and on. You have said that God allows these things and works them together for good, but that is a pretty tough thing to ask of people for the 70+ years they live on this earth. Heaven may be real but it's difficult to think about such things when your life is a real hell on earth.

Jeff: I must confess, Jucinda, that your question has disturbed me for quite some time. Again, however, when you think about it, this is the only possible scenario in which genuine, authentic, love can exist.

Jucinda: Yes, Jeff, but this seems like an awfully high price to pay for love.

Jeff: If love were temporary, then I would have to agree. But when you compare what we are often called to endure here on the earth with what God has promised to grant those who choose to love him, then, the difference is astounding. The scales are so lopsided that God truly maintains His integrity while accomplishing His ultimate purposes in this world.

Jucinda: What do you mean?

Jeff: Well, imagine that the first day of a new year the following things happened to you. You woke up only to discover that you needed a root canal. On your way to the dentist you totaled your car. While waiting for the tow truck and a taxi, your unwed sixteen-year-old calls you to tell you that she is pregnant. When the taxi finally arrives, you find your husband riding in the cab, informing you that he lost his job. While in the dentist's chair, your son calls to tell you that he has been kicked out of school for marijuana use. You arrive home just after your painful appointment with the dentist to discover that your house has burned down and that, due to a lack of income, your husband had to cancel the insurance. As you fall asleep in a hotel room that night, the phone rings one last time to tell you that your parents, while driving down to visit, were in an accident and are seriously injured lying in the hospital. Now that is a bad day!

Jucinda: (laughing) Yes, I would have to agree.

Jeff: But what if the other 364 days of that year were just brilliant? On January 2, you win the lottery. Two hundred and fifty thousand dollars a year for the next thirty years! Then, you receive a call informing you that your blood type is extremely rare and that you can lose weight by doing two things: one, by avoiding exercise; and two, by eating all the chocolate you possibly can. Next, as you are sitting by the pool (remember, January is summer in Australia) sipping your favorite drink, your cardiologist phones to let you know that the tests are back and that your heart is that rare type of heart that makes for a long and productive life. As each day passes in that new year, the news just gets better and better.

Jucinda: OK, OK, what is your point?

Jeff: Well, Jucinda, if I met you on January first of the following year and ask you how your previous year went, you would say, "Absolutely wonderfully! My whole life has changed!" I would then reply, "But I heard you had a horrible January first! They told me your house burned down, your children were in trouble, and your husband got fired." My guess is that you would respond, "Well, yes, that is true. I had a very painful day, but when compared with the rest of the year, that was all small stuff. That year was the most fantastic year of my existence!" Do you think that's true, Jucinda?

Jucinda: Yes, I suppose so.

Jeff: In a similar fashion, if you compare our life on earth with our life in heaven with a loving God, a life that will last forever, the goodness we will experience there will far outweigh any pain we are called upon to endure here. I am not belittling the pain and suffering that is ever present in the lives of so many people. Indeed, we all have our burdens—whether physical or mental—to bear. But for those who choose to use their freedom to pursue this loving relationship with God, no amount of suffering here can compare with the overwhelming bliss He has promised to those who love Him. And remember,

Jucinda, the primary way in which the pain in this world can decrease is for men and women everywhere to make a resolution to use their freedom in a healthy and productive fashion where people love their neighbors as themselves. Alternatively, God could severely lessen the pain by removing the free will of every human being. But since free will is essential to authentic love, God is simply not going to choose this path. However, God will greatly reward those who have chosen to use their freedom to enter into life's ultimate relationship.

Again, there is a verse in the Bible which communicates this idea. "I consider that our present sufferings are not worth comparing with the glory that will be revealed in us" [Romans 8:18].

While I have often thought of the application of this verse into our lives, I am forever indebted to Lee Strobel, award winning journalist with the Chicago Tribune, for bringing it to life and solidifying my understanding. He writes:

> *We should not deny the reality of our pain in this life. It might be terrible. It might be chronic. It might go on for all seventy-two of your years. But in heaven, after 5,484,545 days of pure bliss, and with an infinite more to come—if someone asked, "So, how has your existence been?" you'd instantly react by saying, "It has been absolutely wonderful! Words can't describe the joy and the delight and the fulfillment!" If they said, "But didn't you have a tough time before you got here?" you would probably think back and say, "Well, yes, it's true that those days were painful, I can't deny that. But when I put them in the context, in light of all God's outpouring of goodness to me, those bad days aren't even worth comparing with the eternity of blessings and joy that I've experienced."*[23]

As Jucinda contemplated my comments, the mood around the table was noticeably solemn. I decided that this was the perfect time to make one final suggestion with regard to the manner in which God deals with us during life's most trying times.

Embracing the Light

Any honest evaluation of the human race yields an undeniable conclusion: *those who have suffered greatly often have the greatest impact upon the rest of us.* Scottish theologian James Stewart once said, "The fact is that it is the world's greatest sufferers who have produced the most shining examples of unconquerable faith."[24] Corrie Ten Boom's horrific experiences in the Nazi death camps spurred her toward a worldwide ministry of forgiveness and reconciliation. As she traveled from place to place, Corrie told others how she was able to forgive those who had been so cruel to her. This does not seem possible. How on earth could a person possibly forgive someone who had been responsible for the death of a father, mother, and sister? Even more astounding, however, is Corrie's insistence that the love of God was present in this hellish situation. "No pit is so deep that God's love is not deeper still," became a popular quote attributed to Corrie. Corrie's story, as well as thousands of others, including my own, led me to hold two firm convictions on this matter.

One, people who endure great trials seldom believe that God is the cause or that He is uncaring. Peter Kreeft sheds an eye-opening light on this issue when he says,

> It is significant to note that most of the objections to the existence of God from the problem of suffering come from outside observers who are quite comfortable, whereas those who actually do the suffering are made into stronger believers by their suffering.[25]

Having lived in Africa for a time, I can tell you that this is not the exception, but the rule. The experience of pain seems to catalyze a greater understanding concerning what is real and what is superficial, what is temporary and what is eternal, what is trifling and what is important.

Two, those who come victoriously out on the other side of suffering seldom boast about their own sense of strength, but instead, point to someone beyond themselves. Something about pain draws one closer to the realization that there is someone beyond this world who gives strength to the afflicted.

The point is this: *God does not sit idly by and expect the object of pain to endure hardship alone.* Instead, He gives something that sustains the life of the one called to suffer. God gives His prevailing presence! He grants His supernatural strength to the one who looks to Him for staying power. The Corrie ten Booms of the world stood up and shouted this from the mountaintops. But I wonder how many are listening.

David, one of the authors of the most read book in human history proclaims, "Yea, though I walk through the valley of the shadow of death, I will fear no evil . . . thy rod and thy staff they comfort me" (Psalm 23:4, KJV). David also writes, "The LORD is close to the brokenhearted and saves those who are crushed in spirit" (Psalm 34:18, NIV). And Paul, undeniably a persecuted man, wrote,

> For I am convinced that neither death nor life . . . neither the present nor the future . . . nor anything else in all creation, will be able to separate us from the love of God that is in Christ Jesus our Lord. (Romans 8:38)

In Charles Dickens' classic story, *A Tale of Two Cities*, there is a scene where two prisoners are being carted out to face the guillotine. The first prisoner is a man who is laying down his life for another. He had found his own redemption and was choosing to express man's greatest love by sacrificing his life that another may live. As a result of his decision, he did not face his death with fear and trembling but with an unexplainable peace and serenity. The second prisoner, a little girl, noticed his gentleness and courage and asked, "If I ride with you, will you let me hold your hand? I am not afraid, but I am little and weak, and it will give me more courage."

As they stood on the platform only minutes away from their deaths, the little girl looked up into the welcomed stranger's eyes and said, "I think you were sent to me by heaven."

James Stewart reminds us of this scene when he challenges us to consider that the answer to the mystery of suffering is not an exhaustive explanation but a reinforcing presence that stands by your side during the difficult trials of life.

Glorious Gloria

Never have I seen this illustrated so clearly and powerfully as in the life of a young African lady named Gloria. Growing up in Bulawayo she was the cream of the crop and the pride of her family. Exuberant, funny, and intelligent, she succeeded in whatever she did. A deep thinker and persistent questioner, Gloria would not rest until she found satisfactory answers to her troubling questions. A mutual friend invited Gloria to one of my lectures in which I was highlighting the evidences for both the existence of God and the reality of heaven. Gloria desperately wanted to believe, but there were simply too many unanswered questions. She did, however, continue to come and listen to the evidence until finally one weekend, this talented, intellectual, go-for-broke lady took the plunge and decided that the evidences for God were simply too apparent to ignore. What makes Gloria's story so compelling is that only a few months after crossing over into this new life, she was diagnosed with cancer and was given only a short time to live.

Those who did not know her well believed that the cancer would shake her faith and that she would perhaps denounce what she had previously affirmed. Nothing could have been further from the truth. The transformation that took place in Gloria's life was astounding. At first, she was convinced that God was going to heal her. "I know God is powerful and will rip this cancer right out of me," she would proclaim. Yet with each passing day Gloria became more and more ill. Her cancer was a most aggressive kind that would indeed take her life within just a few short months.

Near the end of her life, I sat by her bed concerned that she was not facing the reality of what was happening to her. Holding her hand I nervously began a dissertation that was meant to be encouraging. Before I could complete my thoughts, however, Gloria interrupted me with words that have been indelibly impressed upon my conscience.

"Jeff," she said, "Do not worry or fear for me. I am OK. Thank you so much for introducing God to me. Had I not known Him, I would have been unable to make it through this time." As I gazed into her eyes, I am sure she noticed my amazement concerning the depth of her faith. Then, she softly whispered something I will never forget.

Squeezing my hand she said, "Jeff, I know Him in a way that you never will, unless you walk the road I am presently on." With that Gloria fell asleep, and the next day she passed away. That was almost twenty years ago, and it is the pattern I have seen in the lives of those who have been called upon to endure such tragic circumstances. Does God reveal Himself in a very special way to those whose hardships seem unbearable to the rest of us? I believe that He does. In fact, the greater the intensity of our suffering, the greater the revelation God gives of Himself. What is beyond and unknown seems to come close in an attempt to reveal what is yet to come. Is this a coincidence, or is this God refusing to sit on His hands? Only the latter seems tenable.

A Quick Application

What about you? To whom do you run when the storms of life come? No doubt, they will come. The real question is, "How will you respond?" For those who have placed their trust in God, an amazing resilience and an unexplainable peace can occur. As we have shown, their examples are compelling.

But why does such peace come? Does it come because of a guarantee that everything will turn out well? No. There is no guarantee that some of the storms of life will not kill us. As long as freedom exists in this world, death could come to any of us anytime and anywhere. If not death, pain. Believing in God does not give you a free pass from pain, suffering, or even death. The world is what it is.

However, the fact that God is willing to walk us through the valley of difficult times is an existential reality. Peace comes to those who have used their freedom to enter into a relationship with God because contentment in every circumstance is the result of such a relationship. Contentment comes not because you feel protected against all potential disaster but because you know who is in charge of this universe and your pain will be used by God to accomplish His purposes in the world. Living your life for a purpose greater than yourself brings enormous freedom and satisfaction.

That is why it is so crucial to determine for what purpose you are living. The answer will indeed determine your response to the trials of your life.

Chapter Seven

Why Does God Restrict My Freedom?

*F*or several moments the room was quiet. Laura's continued tears led me to believe that whatever her pain, it was too deep and personal to share with the group. Many were lost in contemplation, perhaps thinking of people they had loved and lost. At this point I would have been quite willing to grab some leftovers and call it a night. But no one seemed to want to leave. They were in the midst of trying to resolve the most important issue of their lives, and they knew it. Some were reconsidering the possibility that God may indeed exist and perhaps had gotten a bum wrap! Others believed in a higher power but were not convinced that God actually created all things, was personal, and wanted to be involved in their day-to-day affairs.

A few, however, no doubt the silent minority at this point, showed signs of frustration over this new information which had surfaced. They would not be happy until God was debunked! For them, it did not seem like an issue of evidence but one of pragmatism. They did not want God to exist. His existence might lead to other unfortunate and undesirable truths. The passion, therefore, to turn the tide before it was too late, prompted a select few to raise the volume of the conversation and go immediately for the jugular.

12 P.M. and feeling the heat . . .

Barry, a nonparticipant up until this moment, recognized that most of my quotes had come from the Bible. He interrupted the silence and accusingly belted out, "Jeff, you are a Christian aren't you?"

"Yes I am," I said, "Why?"

"Because you Christians are the reason so many people do not believe in God."

"Really?" I said, "What do you mean?"

He responded, "You Christians talk about the love, acceptance, and grace of God in one breath, and then in the next breath talk of how God is going to punish those who do not live by His rules. This does not sound like love and kindness to me. Besides, *why would a good and loving God give so many rules and regulations* that seem intent on preventing us from enjoying our lives?"

With the mood quickly changing, I looked back across the table toward Barry and asked him the same question I had previously asked both Dan and Richard. "Can we engage in a bit of conversation?" With his permission, I continued. "Barry" I asked, "are you suggesting that every person should be able to do whatever he or she wants to do?"

We have already shown the flaw in this argument. One might make such a claim but soon finds himself undermining his own thinking. Remember Hitler? Why should he not be allowed to do what he wants to do without the rest of the world judging him? What about Mugabe? Milosovich? Mussolini?

"Barry," I asked, "in your heart-of-hearts you really do not believe that morality is left up to the individual, do you?"

"Perhaps not," said Barry "but what right does God have to tell us how we should live? You talk about freedom. That's not real freedom!"

"Wait a minute, Barry" I demanded, "Are you suggesting that freedom means no boundaries?"

"Yes," he said.

"Would you consider yourself free right now?" I asked.

"Absolutely; I can do whatever I want," he claimed.

"No, you can't," I demanded. "You can't pull out a gun and shoot everyone around this table, can you? You can't put arsenic in everyone's food and watch them die, can you? You can't go up to the top of this hotel and throw boulders onto the passing vehicles below, can you?" Anticipating his response I was not disappointed when he jumped in with, "Yes! I can! I can do all of those things!"

"True," I responded. "But you can't do them without consequences?"

I continued, "If you shoot all of us, you will surely be shot or go to prison. If you put arsenic in everyone's food, you will be arrested and punished accordingly. If you throw rocks from the top of this hotel building, you will surely be taken into custody and charged with a felony. Therefore, are you truly free? Yes, but with freedom comes responsibility; and the rules of any society are not meant to bind the people but to protect them from one another, and in some cases, from themselves."

Laboring the point I said, "The presence of law does not mean the absence of freedom. Neither does freedom mean the absence of law."

Dan, who had been momentarily awakened by Barry's question, sat up in hope that perhaps this would be the first nail in God's coffin. A career in law enforcement however made it extremely difficult for him to sympathize with Barry's argument,

"OK, Jeff, what is your point?" Barry demanded.

"My point is that God is in no way less loving, less gracious, less merciful by setting down the principles by which we are to live. In fact, the opposite is true. When God gives the moral law, He is motivated by loving kindness."

"Wait a minute, Jeff," Barry rebutted, "how can preventing me from doing the things I want to do possibly be classified as loving kindness?"

Parental Dilemmas

While pausing to breathe I thought of an effective illustration that would once again reveal how most parents engage in a similar activity and call it "love."

Does a father show a lack of love toward his son by demanding the completion of homework? On the contrary, who would dare describe a parent who sets no standards and lays down no rules in the home as a "loving" parent? Rules are not the enemy of love; they are an expression of it. When my father demanded that those who live under his roof refrain from drugs, be home by a certain time, and respect authority, was he expressing hate?

The problem with our generation is that we are like screaming children who have been told not to play in the street. We ignore the rule, get hit by a car, and then in a move that must seem idiotic to God, we scream, "Why, God? Why did You allow this to happen to us? Why?"

In the same way that a good and respectable parent's rules are motivated out of love and protection, so also does the Father of the universe set down His decrees. His law is not arbitrary. He does not give us the law by which to live because He possesses a Hitler-type complex wishing to show us that He is the big, bad boss!

No, His rules stem from the fact that, as Creator and sustainer of the universe, He knows how we as humans are meant to function. He understands what is truly best for us and conversely what will destroy us. Would He be a God of love if He were to sit idly by without communicating to us what is harmful and what spurs a healthy, prosperous life? As Americans continue to remove social and moral boundaries, it would be wise perhaps to stop and ask why the boundaries are there in the first place.

It is interesting that most of our common-day law has its roots in the principles found in the Ten Commandments; stealing, murdering, bearing false witness, cheating, coveting what someone else possesses to the point of action, and even adultery[26] are all illegal actions in the United States. These laws are meant for the protection of the public and are motivated out of empathy for humanity. There is something intrinsic within the heart of man that tells him that murder, lying, and theft are immoral.

Incidentally, the secular-humanist denies absolute morality while categorically stating that right and wrong should be left to the individual (notice the absolute moral statement) and that the only real "wrong" is when someone makes a decision that hurts or wounds someone else. Under such pretenses, a few questions must be considered.

First, is hurting someone absolutely wrong? What happened to no moral absolutes? Second, how exhaustive is the category of hurt? Is it merely physical hurt, or does it also include mental and psychological pain? Under the latter grouping, would things like adultery be considered immoral? After all, the one who has been cheated on usually feels a great sense of pain and loss.

If we are honest with ourselves we would admit that we like the universal law of good and evil. We enjoy living under its protection. However, when the law scrutinizes our life and we are brought to accountability under its light, we want to denounce the absolute moral law and say, "Right and wrong are a personal preference." This is precisely why people often struggle with the Bible. They enjoy all the good stuff but have great difficulty embracing the ordinances which they themselves violate.

However, it has been my experience that once a person understands that God's law is not arbitrarily given, such law is wholeheartedly embraced. Many endorse the moral law not because they are radicals or because they are of a pharisaical bent. They do so because they know that the love of God has created the boundaries within which we should live. These boundaries are for our protection and have been designed to point the way to a happy and productive life.

I find it ironic that most of Jesus' Sermon of the Mount recorded in Matthew 5–7 contains these same boundaries. Yet, this message has been long considered by secular authorities as one of the most profound and life-changing messages of literary antiquity. One psychiatrist described this famous sermon in the following way:

> If you were to take the sum total of all authoritative articles ever written by the most qualified of psychologists and psychiatrists on the subject of mental hygiene, if you were to combine them and refine them and leave out the excess verbiage, if you were to take the whole of the meat and none of the parsley, and if you were to have these unadulterated bits of pure scientific knowledge concisely expressed by the most capable of living poets, you have an awkward and incomplete summation of the Sermon on the Mount.

Imagine. Mental, emotional, and psychological health is the result of living within the confines established by a loving Creator. The truth is that for many Christians, love for people and an understanding that God's law will ultimately protect the innocent, motivates them to stress the morality found in the Bible.

Granted, not everything that glitters is gold. Many Christians have failed miserably in this arena. Rather than expressing God's law in love, some use it as a legalistic whip to punish those who fail to keep the smallest detail of every prohibition. What a tragedy! But remember the example Billy Graham recited to Larry King. Not every plane crashes. Many take off beautifully, fly without incident, and land safely at their destination.

The point of all this is that God gave us the law so that we could live a life of peace, contentment, joy, and satisfaction. The law is not meant to bind us but to free us. When we live within the confines of His law, we are free to really live, trusting that life within the ropes will save us, and others, from so much despair. The law of God, then, is effective in deterring so much that is evil in our world.

The Cry for Justice

I have a friend who is one of the top school teachers in New Zealand. From Scottish roots, his intellect is sharp and his wit and humor adorable. He once told me about a sixteen-year-old bully who was allowed to wreak havoc in his school. An aggressive, verbally abusive lad, this young man was constantly physically wounding numbers of males and females with whom he came into contact. My friend believed that in the interest of the school, he, who had been given every opportunity to change, should be expelled from school. "Seeing the magnitude of his crimes is the only way to get through to this culprit!" he complained.

Indeed, the parents of young sixteen-year-olds throughout the school were dealing with their own issues as they desperately tried to encourage their own children to continue going to school despite their fears of this barbaric bully. So, on the one side, we have twenty to thirty traumatized young men desperately afraid to go to school and wondering why life is so tough. On the other hand, we have a large, aggressive, teenager in a man's body who unfortunately gets his thrills by throwing his weight around. What should be done?

Things finally came to a head when, during a faculty meeting, one teacher stood up and said, "We can't expel this young man. We must show some sympathy and find out why he expresses himself in such a horrific fashion."

After a moment of silence my friend stood and responded, "What about sympathy for the other twenty-five students whose lives have been horrifically affected by this young tyrant?" The boy was expelled, peace was restored, and learning continued. Common sense won out in the end, a rarity these days.

Backyard Brawl

My oldest brother Timothy taught me this valuable lesson when we were playing baseball in the yard one hot summer afternoon. Throughout the summer Timothy had become increasingly frustrated with my younger brother Tony. Tony's immense talent was only superseded by his lackadaisical attitude toward basically everything in life. Having Tony on your baseball team could be good or bad depending on which Tony showed up, the talented one or the apathetic one. To place Tim and Tony on the same team was a mistake. So we avoided such a scenario. However, having them compete against each other could also bring an undesirable outcome. Tim wanted to win but lacked the talent. Tony could easily win but lacked the motivation. Tony's effort that day started off small and tapered off with each new inning. Everyone on the field, including all the neighborhood kids who had joined us, sensed that something was brewing. By the third inning the name calling and verbal abuse had begun, but not by Tim, by Tony. Tim was the quiet type who typically kept his anger inside. His only release came in the form of glaring stares toward the one to whom his wrath was directed. The situation intensified until the bottom of the seventh (the final inning in Vines backyard baseball) when Tim's team came to bat with a legitimate chance of winning the game. As Tim's team readied themselves to bat, something that had occurred hundreds of times before was about to occur again. Tony, knowing how much a victory would mean to Tim, slowly began to sneak away, committing the unpardonable sin of leaving the field before the game was over.

Just as Tim turned around to gather his team, he saw Tony running toward the basement of our home, looking like a man on an unholy mission.

Knowing immediately Tony's intentions, Tim picked up a wooden bat thinking that perhaps he could stop his younger brother in his tracks. From the moment I saw Tim collect the weapon, time seemed to move in slow motion. With a slight hesitation I could see that Tim was carefully considering two things.

First, he was mentally measuring the distance between the bat he held in his hands and the moving target, Tony.

Second, Tim had brought out a pair of mental scales and was weighing the pleasure of nailing Tony with the baseball bat over and against the resulting punishment administered by my father when he arrived from work.

This was a tough comparison. Such an act would not be a misdemeanor tried before the mother court. No, this would be a felony that would have to go before Dad's high court of justice. With time running out (Tony was almost out of firing range), Tim took the baseball bat, held it high in the air, and heaved it some twenty-five yards in Tony's direction. As Tony moved towards the basement, with his head turned defiantly away from Tim, he did not see the ensuing missile.

Unfortunately for Tim, Murphy's Law was in full effect. As soon as the bat left his hand, realizing the potential for disaster, Tim wanted it back. But it was too late. Flying end over end in the shape of a helicopter flying on its side, everyone on the playground could see that the missile was firmly locked onto its target. When the bat struck Tony in the back, he dropped like a wounded duck, quacking just as loud. "Oh!" Tony cried, "I'm hurt! You wounded me for life!" (Tony also had a flair for the dramatic).

Although deeply bruised and wounded, we could determine by the sound of his voice that he would live. While my brother Tim gained an indescribable sense of satisfaction out of what he did, if you were to speak to him today, he would tell you that he wished he had never done such a horrible thing. In fact, the punishment Dad handed down is unknown to this day. Only Dad and Tim are aware of the sentence served. Whatever it was, however, must have been unbearable. For it was enough to discourage Tim from ever touching my brother Tony again.

At the heart of the issue is our failure to acknowledge how the mind works. When we are young, we learn an invaluable truth that seems to be forgotten by the time adulthood rolls around. *As children we learn that if we disobey a rule, consequences will follow.* It is the universal principle of reaping and sowing. This intrinsic understanding forces us, when tempted to act in an unbecoming fashion, to consider the ramifications. If I carry through with this, what will happen?

This conscious activity serves as the most effective deterrent known to man. Freedom does not mean getting to do what you want to do without consequences, so, before we act, we are supposed to think. If we don't, the consequences come. This reality was originally designed to be the most effective deterrent to evil.

Still No Food

My new acquaintances at the hotel found this story to be quite humorous and had not missed the point of the tale. When a potential offender knows that he will have to give an account for his actions and that the penalty he will have to pay for his crimes will be consistent with the degree and intensity of the crime, he will think twice before acting upon his deep-seated emotions of hate and selfishness.

Tim was not a repeat offender because he was well aware of the price he would have to pay. The penalty became the greatest deterrent toward future law-breaking. For Tim, standing before Dad and giving an account of his actions was not worth the temporary satisfaction of committing the crime.

The point in all of this is twofold: first, without serious ramifications to serious crimes, the criminal will in no way be deterred from potential acts of violence; second, the lawmakers of the land are well aware that while the law is good, every detail of it cannot be enforced. There is a sense in which it appeals to the public to act with integrity. Coupled together, these two ideas serve as the most effective deterrent to criminal activity. When the conscience works effectively to remind us of our duty to do that which we ought to do, and, the punishment for doing that which is wrong is consistent with the seriousness of the crime, less crime will be committed. If lawmakers on the earth depend upon both these issues to keep the peace and to protect the innocent, two questions emerge. One, from where does such an idea come? Two, would God be considered unjust in operating His universe by a similar system? After all, God, much more so than the lawmakers of our land, desperately wants to protect the innocent and see good and right prevail. So, the question becomes, "How does God achieve this without violating our free will?"

A Quick Application

Have you ever been strongly convicted about an activity in which you were about to engage? You just knew that what you were considering was inappropriate? How did you respond? Did you stop to think about the consequences?

Have there been times in your life when you found yourself in deplorable circumstances and complained, "Where are you, God?" only to realize that the situation in which you currently resided was the result a bad decision you had made in the past?

In twenty plus years of counseling I have often seen this scenario: a husband cheated on his wife and now his children hate him. So he comes into my office and asks, "Why is my life so bad? Why doesn't God do something?"

A teenager, against his better judgment, takes the drugs offered by a companion. He overdoses and dies. His parents come into my office and say, "Where is God? Why did He allow this to happen?"

A woman has too much to drink. She gets into her car and drives through a stop sign, running over a young child on a bicycle. When she awakens from the coma and discovers what has happened, she complains that God does not love her and has abandoned her. She continues as she exclaims, "Where was God? Why did He allow this to happen?"

Each case stated above is not a hypothetical situation. These events occur every day in our world, and each occurred in my own life! In each situation there was a point at which an internal warning pressed heavily against the conscience of the perpetrator. Unfortunately, the signs were ignored, the consequences not weighed, and evil, pain, and suffering, came as a result.

If you are mad at God over some unfortunate event in the past, reconsider the cause of the occurrence and then truly ask yourself, "Is God the cause of my pain, or did someone else ignore God's great deterrent to evil, the conscience, and commit an act of great injustice?"

Remember, God could remove every potentially painful event from your life, but to do so would require the removal of free will. Since free will is essential to love, God is simply not willing to do that. You and I, however, can minimize the pain around us by keeping the laws we know to be right and avoiding activities we know to be wrong. This takes incredible fortitude and endurance. The temptation to fulfill our desires in an illegitimate fashion is powerful and often relentless. Yet, the safety and security of those we love depends upon our willingness to stand strong. Before we complain to God that His world is a horrible place to live, perhaps we should do two things. One, think about all the pleasurable experiences our existence in God's creation brings. Second, realize that we can make this world so much better by simply doing what we ought to do.

Chapter Eight

God's Ultimate Response to Evil

1 A.M. and all is not well . . .

All this talk about "right" and "wrong," justice and punishment, crime and deterrence, sparked a look of concern in Jucinda's eyes. I noticed Jucinda was fired up and ready to go. She looked to me like a school girl who had the correct answer to the teacher's question. She leaned toward me, waited for an opening, and then bolted in with, "Jeff, I know where you are going with this. I have been waiting for this all night. You are about to tell us that God is going to hold evil men and women accountable for their rebellious violations. Am I right?"

"Jucinda, think about what you are demanding from God. On the one hand, you point the accusative finger at God and ask, "Why do you permit all this evil in the world?" Then, when God responds, "Be patient, justice will come to all those who have used their freedom to hurt and wound others," you become uncomfortable with a God who exacts punishment upon the evildoer. You place God in a no-win situation. You want Him to do away with evil but give Him no options to complete such a task."

I continued, "In reality, the human race wants a God who prevents the possibility of evil in the here and now while at the same time granting human freedom. This scenario is logically impossible. When we are told that God will hold all evildoers accountable for their actions, we criticize God and call Him 'unloving.'

"Jucinda, for this world to make any sense at all there has to be some form of justice, beyond manmade laws and punishment, attached to it. Right?

"Who is going to call the Hitlers, Stalins, Mussolinis, and Mugabes to the high court of justice? Who is going to hold each member of the Third Reich responsible for legislating, inflicting, and overseeing the evils perpetrated upon one race of people? Certainly, The Nuremburg Trials may have brought some to justice but countless others escaped any form of retribution. They will not, however, avoid the day of accountability when each of us faces our Creator."

Jucinda fired back, "Come on, Jeff. Get to the point. Stop avoiding the issue. I know, as well as everyone else around this table that you are talking about hell. You are saying that God is going to send some people to hell. I know that is what you Christians believe. 'Fess up!"

"Yes, Jucinda, I do believe in a place called 'hell,'" I responded.

"Ha! Ha!" she said, "This is the moment I have been waiting for. I knew this was too good to be true! There is no way you can harmonize God with this place the church keeps preaching about called hell! No way! *How on earth could a good God send people to a place of punishment?"*

Surmising that this was a sensitive issue with most of those present, I proceeded with caution.

"Jucinda, can you tell me what you think 'hell' really is? What is it like?" I asked.

"I can tell you exactly what it is like." She said, "It is a place where you burn and burn and burn and where worms eat your flesh and where there is darkness and suffering more horrific than any Nazi concentration camp ever thought about being! This is twelve years of Catholic school talking!"

Catching her breath she continued, "I know what you Christians claim about hell, and there is no way I could ever believe in a God who would send anybody to a place like that!"

Settling down with yet another sip of Diet Coke I began my response by asking Jucinda to consider what the Bible actually teaches about hell. True, the word translated "hell" comes from the Greek word *gehenna*, the name for a place just outside Jerusalem where the bodies of criminals and/or poor citizens were gathered and burned. The smoke from 'gehenna' ascended endlessly from this horrible pit and would have been one of the most detestable sights in Jerusalem.

It should not surprise us then that Jesus, when looking around for an earthly symbol to describe what eternity without God would be like, chose the death and devastation of *gehenna*. My purpose here is not to talk about whether or not a person really burns in hell but instead to illustrate what Jesus taught about hell. He described it with the worst possible symbols imaginable to man.

When speaking of hell, Jesus continually pointed to one primary truth. Yes, hell is an undesirable place. Yes, *hell is not the place God wants anyone to go. But the worst possible thing about hell is that it is the ultimate separation from God.*

I reminded Jucinda that God places such a high value on our free will that even if such freedom opens the door to the possibility of evil, He is willing to take the risk. The highest value of the universe must be protected at all cost. We had thoroughly established this in the course of the evening.

But then I asked, "Now if free will is such an issue in this world, will free will not be equally important in the world to come?"

When confronted with this possibility Jucinda asked, "What do you mean?"

"Well," I replied, "If a person spends his entire life wrapped up in his own selfish ambitions and selfish pursuits—refusing to pursue a relationship with the Creator, in thanksgiving and worship for all He has provided—would God be unfair and unjust to grant him the ultimate ramifications of personal freedom?

"In other words, if a man's greatest desire is to live in a world void of God, His commandments, His morality, or any other thing associated with Him, would God be unjust by granting the person his wish?

"Imagine that no matter how many times God pursues you, convicts you, draws you toward Himself, your response is always the same. Internally, you say, 'I don't want God. I don't need God. I do not want a universe like that.' Would God not be the ultimate respecter of free will if He did not force Himself upon you, especially eternally speaking, but simply placed you in a realm whereby He would separate the two of you forever?"

C.S. Lewis, one of the greatest thinkers of our time described this scenario when he painted a picture of the day of accountability. He describes how the selfish, godless person approaches the throne of God and then, in a moment of frustration, God throws His hands up in the air and exclaims, "All right then, not My will but yours be done!"[27]

Jucinda sat stunned, once again considering the ramifications of a free-will universe. Claiming hell as a place where God allows a person the full ramifications of her earthly free-will decisions, caught Jucinda off guard. I pressed, "Does God respect free will to such a degree that He would allow a person who wished Him out of existence to live as though He were not around?" This was the question with which Jucinda began to struggle.

While Jucinda sat contemplating and Laura sat weeping, I asked the others to imagine what the world would be like if God were to completely withdraw His influence. If God withdrew His internal system of deterrence, if evil had no restraint, if God really sat on His hands, what would the world look like? I stressed to the crowd that, when talking about hell, this is the primary point Jesus was making. Completely remove God and you completely remove the possibility of anything good. Indeed, this type of world would be a horrible place to live. Indeed, it would be a living hell.

The reality that one day we will face God and be held accountable for the manner in which we have used our free will continues to serve as God's primary deterrence to evil. When we think we may hide our violations from men, there is still God who sees everything, works through the conscience, and holds everyone accountable.

Moreover, in a very real sense, hell is God's way of granting the logical ramifications of man's ultimate free-will decision to live in the type of universe for which he has been yearning. I cannot begin to imagine what a place like that would be. Yet, if that is what man insists on possessing, the ultimate respecter of free will will grant that which even He Himself opposes.

More than Deterrence

"Are you saying that hell is nothing more than God allowing man's fullest expression of His free will?" replied Jucinda.

"No," I said "but this indeed is a major part of it."

"OK," she responded, "What's the other part?"

"Justice," I said.

"According to the Bible, God is not merely a God of love but also a God of holiness and purity. I do not think this concept would be difficult for humanity to grasp. If God were indeed God, He should be holy and pure. He should keep His own law perfectly, never violating a single ordinance. In fact, God's character should go far beyond merely *keeping* the law. God's motivations and thoughts should be totally pure as well."

Jucinda responded, "So, God is pure and holy; what does this have to do with hell?"

"According to the Bible," I said, "in the same way that God's love requires Him to honor free will, His holiness requires Him to punish all sin."

"Wait a minute!" she interrupted. "Why can't God just forgive our sin?"

Pausing to think about her request I asked, "If Hitler's atrocities were recounted one by one at the Nuremburg trials, with Jewish parents who had lost children in the gas ovens watching with intent, and, then, in a cruel twist, the judge dropped the gavel and said; 'That's OK, Hitler, old buddy—you are forgiven. You are free to go,' would that be justice?"

"No, I guess not." she replied.

"Well," I said, "Although our sin may not be that big of a deal to us, to God it is cosmic treason! All sin ultimately hurts someone who has been made in the image of God. For God to completely ignore our offenses would be a serious violation of justice, as well as a direct attack upon His holy character."

With Laura raising her head and paying special attention to this part of the discussion I continued: "Our sin does something to God of which most people are not aware. According to the Bible, when we violate God's law, our sin creates a tension between the two aspects of God's nature: His love and His holiness.

"When God sees our rebellion, His justice says we must be punished, but the other side of His nature, God's love, desperately desires to forgive us. This tension is the catalyst for the most important theological question known to man: when dealing with our sin, how can God remain true to both sides of His nature? How can He punish us and love us at the same time? This is especially disconcerting when we realize that the Bible teaches that the 'wages of sin is death.'"

"Whoa!" exclaimed Sherri. "Are you saying that God is going to kill all of us?"

"Not at all," I replied. "I am simply reminding you that our sin is so serious that, just as it would be a travesty of justice to send Hitler home for the holidays, it would be an equal injustice for God to say, 'Sherri, I know you have violated my law time and time again, but don't worry, be happy, all is well.'

"God cannot turn a blind eye to our sin; such would be a violation of a primary part of His character."

Hold On!

Notice again the contradiction. We accuse God of injustice when evil men are allowed to wreak havoc in the world. Yet as soon as we imply that God has a plan to hold us accountable for our evil actions, we again point the accusative finger and ask, "God, where is the love?"

Jucinda, knowing where all this was leading, said, "OK, Jeff, you said that everybody sins and that our sin creates a tension in the nature of God, putting His love and His holiness at odds. How does He solve the tension?"

Yippee! That is the only way to describe the way I felt when Jucinda asked the million dollar question.

"Ah," I said, "the only answer for this tension is the cross of Jesus Christ." No other religion in the world offers this. Before it is so easily debunked, one ought to take a long, hard look at what this Christian symbol is really all about.

A Quick Application

Have you ever placed God in an unreasonable position? As we discussed above, many accuse God of refusing to deter or prevent evil. However, when we speak of a future day of accountability—God's primary means of deterrence—the skeptic accuses God of being unloving. "How could a loving God punish someone?" we complain.

Placing God in a "no-win" situation does not stop with the major philosophical and theological themes of our day. In the course of

---

day-to-day living, we often make illogical requests of God. We ask God to grant us peace and tranquility while working twelve to fourteen hour days, all in the pursuit of more and more stuff! This ambition to stockpile catalyzes great stress and robs us of much of the joy that comes with living. There is no time for joy or peace! We cannot ask God for peace while living our lives in such a manner as to restrain it. God may show us the way to peace but will not force it upon us.

Similarly, we ask God for good health but refuse to live a life of moderation, carefully managing what we eat and taking advantage of the opportunities to exercise.

After my mother passed away a few years ago, I began praying intensely for my father's health. One day I realized that no matter how much I pray, the fact that my father has smoked cigarettes for most of his life and continues to do so today make it extremely difficult for God to answer my request.

Why? In order for God to prolong my father's life, He would have to remove my dad's freedom to choose whether or not he is going to continue to pump this poison into his lungs. Once again, we have shown that God's rule of thumb for operating in this creation scenario includes a cause-and-effect relationship between man and his freedom. God is not in the habit of coming down in a bolt of lightning and stopping our evil deeds, even if such evil deeds are inflicted upon our own bodies.

I deeply love my father and pray that he will live a long and productive life. He has been a great father! However, if my dad were to pass away due to lung cancer or some other disease related to cigarette smoking, I would not blame God. Even God agrees that in many ways, we are the captain of our ship, and the decisions we make negatively or positively affect our lives.

Ask yourself, "In what practice am I currently involved that is taking away my joy, my pleasure, my life?" We simply cannot live lives that are in direct opposition to everything that promotes health and vitality and then blame God for our pain. What changes do you need to make immediately? Our lives are clearly affected by our choices. What changes do you need to make?

Chapter Nine

The Crux of
the Matter

1:30 A.M. and a new beginning . . .

If Laura was emotionally unstable earlier, as soon as I mentioned the cross of Jesus, she became an emotional wreck! Unsure of how much more of this she could take, I paused in hopes that someone would talk to her. No one came to her aid.

Finally, taking a huge leap of faith that Laura would perhaps respond to me, I asked, "Laura, are you OK?" Looking up, she said nothing but merely raised her hand as if to say, 'Back away, I'll be fine.'

However, she wasn't fine, and everyone knew it. Something was horribly wrong. And just as shocking as her unwillingness to receive help was her willingness to remain at the table. Why did she not simply get up and leave? I just couldn't figure it out. The only reason I could think of was that she wanted or even needed to stick around until she found the answer for which she was desperately searching.

It was at this point that Laura's close friend, Rebecca, asked the final question of the night. Rebecca knew very little about Christianity or God, for that matter, but, she did know the central story of Jesus and could not come to grips with why God or Christians would emphasize a man nailed to a tree. How could this be a story of victory?

Rebecca had managed to remain silent throughout the entire six hours, but now she felt compelled to speak. In her own attempt to discredit Christianity, she asked the ultimate question upon which all other answers rest. She cleared her throat and calmly but arrogantly stated, "Jeff, all this sounds interesting but *what kind of a religion places a crucified man at the center of its belief system?* Jesus was not a success. He was a failure."

> We had been talking about pain, suffering, evil, and justice for hours. Little did we know that the final question of the night would cover the scope of all these issues. Thrilled that the question had been asked, I responded by asking my audience to go back in time with me for a moment and investigate the final hours of Jesus' life. With eager anticipation and their approval, I began the final conversation.

The Final Story

The final hours of Jesus' life are gruesome ones. Arrested in the Garden of Gethsemane, Jesus prays, *"Father, if you are willing, take this cup from me"* (Luke 22:42). The fact that Jesus prayed such a prayer should not surprise us. While traveling throughout the land of Palestine, Jesus would have witnessed many crucifixions. Knowing that within hours He too would face a painful and horrible execution, Jesus began sweating drops of blood (see Luke 22:44). Skeptics often read a verse like this and accuse the writers of the New Testament of being legend makers. Yet "sweating drops of blood" is an authentic medical condition known as *hematidrosis*, the effusion of blood into the perspiration. The condition is caused by extreme anguish where the subcutaneous capillaries dilate and burst mingling blood with sweat. Furthermore, hematidrosis causes the skin to be extremely sensitive to touch. The fact that Jesus only hours later will be scourged by Pilate's soldiers makes His suffering incomprehensible.

Yet the writers of the New Testament—men who have been credited by those who study literary antiquity as "first rate" and "trustworthy" historians—record what happened to this man, Jesus, in an orderly and systematic fashion.

First, Jesus faced the religious leaders of His day. These men were not that impressed with the system of grace and forgiveness Jesus taught. Without the law as a means to save they would be out of a job. Here, Jesus would be beaten with open and closed hands, spat upon, and ridiculed (see Matthew 26:67-68).

Realizing that the religious court did not have the authority to pronounce and carry out the sentence of death upon Jesus, they sent Him to be tried on trumped up charges before the Roman court. Severely weakened by extreme beatings, Jesus stood before Pilate who found Him somewhat offensive but in no way worthy of death.

Passing the buck, Pilate sent Jesus to Herod in the hope that he would solve the issue and restore peace. That Jesus would be constantly beaten during His journeys to and from the various courts is an historical likelihood. Herod, like Pilate, found Jesus interesting but unworthy of capital punishment, so, he sent Him back to Pilate where Pilate eventually had Jesus scourged and handed over for crucifixion.

The fact that Jesus was scourged by Pilate after a night of anguish that included hours without water and relentless, continuous beatings, is something that is crucial to remember. You and I may not be familiar with the scourging process but Jesus would have been all too familiar with what He was about to face.

The word "scourge" is the English translation of the Greek word *phragelloo*, which means, "open bowel." Without being too crass, our English word "flatulence" comes from the Greek word *phragelloo*. More than describing the process of scourging, *phragelloo* is meant to illustrate the result of someone who has endured the beating. The first-century historian, Eusebius, who was an eyewitness to many crucifixions, described a scourging as a severe punishment where

> the sufferer's veins were laid bare, and the very muscles, sinews, and bowels of the victim were open to exposure. The skin and flesh were gashed to the bone in every direction, and where the armed ends of the lashes struck, deep bloody holes were torn.[28]

Eusebius's words confirm the historical fact that, typically, two types of whips were used in a scourging. The first type featured a leather whip with leather sockets attached to the end of seven strands. As the Roman Lector laid the whip onto Jesus' back, those sockets, filled with sharp pieces of bone, were designed to dig into His skin and extract bits of flesh as it was withdrawn.

The second type of whip also featured sockets at the end of leather strands but was filled with metal balls intended to bruise the back, legs, and chest of the victim. Understandably, many criminals died before they ever made it to the cross. Scourging was sometimes referred to as "halfway" death.

Medically speaking, Jesus at some point would have gone into hypovolemic shock where the heart races to pump blood that is not present. Consequently, the blood pressure drops and the victim collapses. Moreover, the kidneys stop producing urine to maintain what volume of fluid remains. Finally, the body becomes unbelievably thirsty craving the fluids to replace the loss of blood volume.

If the victim were to survive, the pain of such torture would only have made the nails of the cross that much more excruciating. As a matter of fact, this whole form of punishment was so intense that a new word had to be coined to describe it. The word, "excruciating" literally means, "out of the cross." Historians agree that no form of execution is as painful and excruciating as crucifixion.

Today, our forms of capital punishment may vary, but in almost all cases the circumstances are highly controlled. Death comes quickly and predictably, and the medical examiners carefully certify the victim's passing. Comparatively, crucifixion is neither quick nor predictable.

After insults, unjust trials, beatings, and a scourging, Jesus was delivered once again to Pilate who handed Him over to the Romans to be crucified. Stripped of His clothes, Jesus would be commanded to carry a beam called a *patibulum*. The *patibulum,* covered with splintered wood and weighing over two hundred pounds, was placed on Jesus' tender and blood-covered back. He would carry this beam, separate from the *vertical beam* that was mounted permanently in the ground, up to Golgotha where the Romans would stretch out his arms, drive five-to-seven-inch-long spikes, tapered to a sharp point, into his wrists or into the place of the median nerve. The nerve would be crushed upon impact. The pain this causes is not comparable to any other impact or trauma. Next, the nails would be driven through Jesus' feet, once again crushing the nerves and sending a shock through the body.

Jesus would have been hoisted as the crossbar was attached to the vertical stake. So, with thorns on his head, a sliced and bare back on a splintered wooden cross, and the stress of simply hanging on a tree, the long, slow, process of death begins. This long, drawn-out death was so despicable that the first-century Stoic, Seneca, preferred suicide over crucifixion. He wrote:

> Can anyone be found who would prefer wasting away in pain, dying limb by limb, or letting out his blood drop by drop, rather than expiring once and for all? Can any man be found willing to be fastened to the accursed tree, long

sickly, already deformed, swelling with ugly weals on shoulders and chest, and drawing the breath of life amid long, drawn-out agony? He would have many excuses for dying even before mounting the cross.[29]

Almost unbearable to watch, bystanders of crucifixions often waited for long hours for death to come. Ultimately, as Dr. Alexander Metherel explains, the victim dies of asphyxiation. In his interview with Lee Strobel in the book *The Case for Christ*, Metherel explains how hanging on the cross places an incredible stress on the muscles and diaphragm as the chest is placed in an inhaled position. Therefore, in order to exhale, the victim must push up with his feet and legs. This eases the tension on the muscles and allows for exhale.

Each time Jesus pushed upwards, however, the nails would tear through the feet eventually locking against the tarsal bones. Jesus' bloodied back would continue to rub up and down the coarse wood of the cross until complete exhaustion set in preventing Him from pushing up in order to breathe. Cardiac arrest would follow and Jesus, after twenty-four hours of relentless, ruthless, and unimaginable suffering, would commend His spirit into His Father's hands.[30]

A Deafening Silence

As the group sat in a stunned silence, Laura, who had sat in quiet desperation for over six hours, broke her silence. She began to sob. Her tears and emotion reminded me of my years in Africa and the loud mourning with which the Shona people express their sorrow. Within seconds all her inhibitions, along with her strong intentions to maintain her composure, had given way to something far more important. Rising from her chair, she passionately confessed to the crowd.

"Please listen," she begged. "What this man is saying is all true! It's all true! This all makes sense. We are all in trouble. We are all running from what we know to be true. *God hates me. He hates me!* I am a failure and He is going to punish me. God help me. God help all of us!"

The puzzlement of her dramatic shift was outdone only by the complexity of her statement that God hated her and was going to "punish her."

What great sin had she committed? What event in her life had the six-hour conversation about God brought to the surface? Visibly shaken by a Laura the staff had never seen, they once again looked to me to resolve this uncomfortable situation. I calmly walked to the other end of the table, knelt before Laura and asked, "What is the matter? Why are you convinced that God is going to punish you?"

Without delay Laura responded, "Because I have been a bad person. I have lived an immoral life for the past twenty years and am in fact, living an immoral life now. I know God is real, and I know He is disappointed with my life. He has been convicting me for a long time now, and I have refused to change. I know my time is coming and that He will punish me for all my wrongdoings. God hates me!"

Puzzled, I asked why she thought God hated her. At this, Laura opened the window of her life and allowed all of us to look in. No words can describe the intensity around the table at this point. The staff had always seen Laura as the consummate professional who would never lose her composure. This straight-laced, success-driven business woman had never before revealed such emotion. Obviously, the conversation that night caused Laura's deepest feelings to surface. She desperately needed help and I began to believe that maybe, just maybe, this entire night had been orchestrated by God to bring her back to Him. Sensing her cry for help I asked again, "Laura, why do you think God hates you?"

Laura told us that when she was younger she felt she could never please her father. No matter what she did, her father never seemed to approve. This was devastating to her. She was a little girl who, more than anything else, sought the approval of her father. By the age of sixteen, convinced that her father would never be pleased with her, she ran away seeking to discover approval somewhere else. Driven to succeed in order to prove to the world that she was worthy of praise, she ran from job to job and man to man.

One season of her life brought her to a man who introduced her to God by way of the church. In her mind, she finally had met a man who loved and valued her in a very special way. Unfortunately, the God to whom Laura was introduced was nothing more than a glorified version of her father—a sword-wielding taskmaster who expected and demanded moral perfection. To be accepted before this god, one must be without sin or blemish and, in fact, live the perfect moral life. It was not very long until Laura became frustrated with her inability to live up to what she believed God demanded of her. No matter how hard she tried, she never felt accepted by this God of perfection. In her mind, it was impossible to please God. He sat up in heaven just waiting to pounce at the first sign of disobedience.

This introduced a crucial point where Laura is concerned. She affirmed that God's law was good. She knew in her heart that a denial of absolute right and wrong made life completely unlivable and, furthermore, that such a law of good and evil was given in order that we may live in harmony with one another and with God. She agreed with the goodness of the law but found that keeping the law perfectly was impossible. She realized that she could never meet the requirements of God's standard, so she did what most people do: give up completely.

When the whole thing became too much to bear, as she had done before, she ran away, once again seeking full acceptance by anyone who would give it. She continued her search, and moved from man to man and relationship to relationship, wanting so desperately to be embraced. For the past twenty years, Laura had been running away from anyone who rejected her in hopes of finding someone who would love her unconditionally. Yet, with every relationship change and every immoral choice, she felt the tug of God on her heart.

Many times she wanted to submit, but fearing rejection she decided that no man would ever have her heart. *If the heart were never given,* she thought, *it could never be broken.*

I wish you could have seen the look on her face when I told her what every person in the universe, who has ever thought about God, needs so desperately to hear. I began to relate once again Jesus' primary message to those who would have ears to hear.

"God is not the heckler in the stands who shouts and ridicules when we drop the ball of morality during the game of life. No. He is the coach in the locker room at halftime who says, 'OK, Jeff. You failed. I know it and you know it. Now get back out there and keep trying to live the life you were meant to live. I am here. Together, we can do this!'"

In a moment of hope, Laura looked at me and asked, "But you said God was holy and that He must punish sin to remain true to His character. How can He just turn a blind eye to my sin? How can He not punish me?"

"Remember," I said, "our sin causes a tension in God's nature that is only resolved at the cross." Laura, deeply interested in every word, continually hoping for the answer to her lifelong dilemma, demanded an explanation when she said, "How does the cross solve this tension?"

"The Bible clearly teaches that where the law is concerned, there are two ways to be righteous," I said. "First, one can be right with the law by simply keeping it to perfection. In other words, if one never breaks the law, he is considered perfect by the law and thus deemed righteous. Second, even if one were to break the law, once the penalty is paid by the lawbreaker, he is once again considered 'right' by the law. This is the very same principle we use today in human law. Once a prisoner has paid his dues to society, he is free to go and deemed righteous until that time in which he violates the law again."

Laura interrupted, "Yes, that's my point! If any of us are righteous, it will not last very long. As soon as we fail again, then will God not condemn us and punish us?"

"No," I replied. "This is where the cross comes in. The cross meets the requirements of God's holiness because it is on the cross where Jesus paid the penalty for your sin and mine. This is why a man who could have worked a miraculous sign and rescued Himself from the execution of the cross chose to remain and die.

"The point is that we may not be able to be righteous under the first option, but, we are able to obtain it under the second. Jesus paid the penalty on our behalf. This is why the cross is seen as the climactic point of human history. It is where the gap between God and man was bridged and where intimacy between Creator and creature is restored. Once the penalty has been paid, by God's own system of justice, we are seen as righteous and no longer deserve condemnation."

"Yes," Laura responded, "I can see that, Jeff, but what about the next time I do the wrong?"

"This again is the beauty of the cross. God decided that Jesus' sacrifice would be a 'once and for all' event. He lived a perfectly sinless life, not deserving death, yet gave His life freely for us. This sacrifice was deemed by God sufficient to forgive past, present, and future sins. Yes, we did (and will continue to do) the crime, but Jesus did the time! This is the constant message given by Jesus and His Apostles" (see Romans 5:1 and 8:1).

Unsurprisingly, awakened from his long slumber, Dan remarked, "Cool. That means we can have a sin free-for-all without fear of punishment!"

"But why would you want to do something that you know is a violation of God's law, especially when you know that His law is not given arbitrarily but is motivated out of love and protection for all people, including ourselves?" I asked.

Once again, Dan wished he had never spoken but, in my heart, I knew that Laura was experiencing a dramatic shift in her thinking and the conversation needed desperately to continue down the present path. So I ignored Dan and looked directly toward Laura and said, "This God who seeks so desperately to love you has provided a way whereby the barriers to relationship with Him can be removed and unconditional love can thrive. This barrier (sin) that once separated you and God has been removed by Jesus' great act on the cross."

Laura's friend interrupted, "OK, Jeff but why a cross? Why all the blood and guts and suffering? Why could God not take care of the issue another way?"

For our readers, this is a question with which I have been presented many times. The answer is: "of course God could have accomplished this any way He chose. This is what it means to be omnipotent. God can do whatever He wants." But this is not the issue. The real issue is, "Why *did* God choose to do it this way? Why did He choose to watch His own Son die a horrible death on the cross as a means to save us from the eternal consequences of our own evil free-will decisions (sin)?"

True, the cross was prophesied hundreds of years before it ever took place. True, the Old Testament sacrificial system was a foreshadowing of what God would accomplish on the cross. But, in reality, God could have accomplished this any way He chose. Yet He chose a cross. Why?

Think about it for a moment. The cross, serving as the most horrific form of suffering known to man, was the perfect way to communicate to man that, although in our minds our sin is not that big of a deal, in the mind of God it is cosmic treason and has catastrophic consequences in the universe. The horror of the cross and the scourging Jesus endured is a graphic reminder that our sin is a serious matter and should be avoided at great costs.

Greater still, the cross resolves the tension in the nature of God. Remember how we stated above that our sin brings tension into the nature of God? He wants to love us, but

His holy nature requires Him to punish us and separate Himself from us? How can God possibly enter into relationship with sinners? Again, how can He love us when we are so unlovable?

The answer is staggering and is found in the cross. On the cross the requirements of God's holiness have been met in that sin has been punished. Similarly, the requirements of His love have been met in that He Himself paid the penalty for our sin. He did for us what had to be done. This is why the Apostle Paul says He did it to become both "just [the law has been upheld] and the one who justifies [He Himself paid the penalty for our sins]" (Romans 3:26).

If I had any doubts that God had arranged this meeting, those doubts faded when Laura, with tears of joy in her eyes said, "Jeff, please tell me. How can I be 'right' with God? How can I get this unconditional acceptance and love?"[31]

The Truth of the Matter

Hours had passed since Dan's first question. The evening had not turned out in any form or fashion in the manner Laura had expected. The failure of anyone to leave at any moment throughout the night assured me that down deep inside we are all looking for an answer that we trust exists.

Many will accuse the religious man of first creating a need and then providing a solution. My experience throughout the world has made such an argument untenable. Present within every race and culture is the idea that there is someone greater than humanity. Is it the hope that someone is watching, or is it, in the words of Pascal, a "God-shaped void" intentionally placed within the heart of man, encouraging man to seek the One who wants desperately to be found?

Rather than choosing to lord His power over the earth and force free-will men and women to submit, *God seems to be about the business of drawing us to Himself, giving us the final say* in whether we will enter into relationship with Him or not. Only then can genuine love, the greatest value in God's creation scenario, be given and received.

Without violating our free will and God's own holiness, the Creator of the universe provided a way whereby each of us can be forgiven our failures, be deemed as holy and acceptable before Him, and be given the right to enter into relationship with the One who launched this whole endeavor.

As I summarized each of these points, I looked toward Laura and said, "Laura, there is only one thing God requires from you." With every head turned toward the south end of the table, Laura replied, "What's that?"

"That you humble yourself, acknowledge your failures, and accept God's provision for your life," I said.

"You mean the cross of Jesus?" she asked.

"Yes." I said. "Everything that needed to be done to make you right with God was done two-thousand years ago on a cross. All God asks of you is to humbly admit your sin and cling to the cross for the forgiveness of past, present, and future sins. Can you do this?"

Without hesitation, right there in the hotel lobby, with onlookers visibly stirred, Laura knelt down and exclaimed, "Yes, Jeff, I not only can but I will! I know I can never be perfect. I have much sin in my life. But I want to be right with God. I want to live for this purpose greater than myself."

Shocked! This is the only way to describe everyone present. As Laura and I prayed together, she tightly squeezed my hand. When she had openly humbled herself and embraced the cross of Jesus, she stood before her staff and proclaimed, "This is it! This is what I have been looking for the past twenty years. You will never find real peace until each of you do this. Please. We know in our hearts that God is real and that He is seeking each one of us. If any barrier exists, please, let's discuss it now. Let's ask our questions and make our commitment together."

The night had passed so quickly. Most were extremely tired. All were shocked and contemplative. After Laura spoke, I wondered if others would make this commitment. Although others would want more dialogue, Laura was the only one to cross the great divide that night. As we left that evening, I reminded my hosts of Jesus' words. Such powerful words came after four hundred years of people wondering if God was still involved in humanity, and if there was a way whereby men and women could restore the broken relationship that seemed to exist between God and man.

This highly anticipated teacher named Jesus stood on a hill in Palestine, waited for the crowd to settle, and began the most famous sermon ever preached with the words that would answer both those questions. He said, "Blessed are the poor in spirit [humble], for theirs is the kingdom of heaven" (Matthew 5:3).

In one fell swoop, the legalism of the Pharisees was denounced and the "way" of God appeared. Righteousness is not found in a list of do's and don'ts but in the person of Jesus Christ and His work on the cross. All who humbly come to Him, accepting this forgiveness, will find peace with God and a new reason for living.

Laura had not only embraced this new life but was quickly becoming a champion for the cause! Around 2 A.M., the group finally shuffled away from the roundtable, each departing to his or her home. I spent a few more minutes with Laura, and then we said our goodbyes.

I found it extremely difficult to sleep that night. I kept wondering if I could have perhaps answered some of the questions in a more complete fashion. Or maybe I could have been more compassionate when dealing with some of the more sensitive issues. A night of tossing and turning led to a new day with a new concern. *What really happened last night? Was all of that real?* I thought to myself. *Did Laura actually make a change or did the emotion of the night lead to a temporary emotional decision?*

Although the night had been long, I knew that Laura would be in the hotel lobby bright and early, so I scurried to the elevator in hopes of meeting her. When the door opened to the lobby, there she was, professionally dressed and ready to meet the day's challenges. When she saw me, she ran over to greet me and immediately began talking about the night she had had with God after our meeting was over. *Yep, the relationship has begun!* I thought to myself. *Laura has walked through the door into the world of great adventure!*

We talked for a little while longer, and then duty called. As she walked away in those expensive high heels, the click clack sound brought back the memories of just fifteen hours ago when Laura was simply seeking some entertainment. What she had found instead was the very thing she had been seeking all of her life: communion with a loving, kind, gracious, and forgiving God who exhibits unconditional love and calls us to an abundant life!

A Quick Application

Remember what we said earlier. God's law is not given arbitrarily. His law is motivated out of love for you and your neighbors. This is why guilt comes! God wants you to seriously consider the consequences of what you are doing. When you break His law, you wound yourself and others, both of whom have been created in the image of God and are precious to Him.

This is why guilt is a universal reality. That does not mean, however, that there is only one way with which to deal with our guilt. Think of the various options available when faced with the guilt experienced when we have spoken harshly to someone we love, mistreated one of our children, selfishly hoarded our resources when we should have given to someone in need, cheated on the golf course, abused a weaker personality, or engaged in any other activity we know to be wrong.

We can ignore the guilt until it goes away. We can claim that our guilt is culturally conferred, that is, that it only comes because we have been culturally conditioned. We can laugh at guilt and believe that it is only a silly emotion. We can even overestimate our own goodness to the point that guilt becomes a nonissue. All are available, but none are sufficient ways of dealing with the guilt we feel when we have violated the moral ethics to which we firmly ascribe.

Only one response to guilt is effective in restoring mental health and vitality. God has planned it this way. It is yet another means by which God draws us to Himself. He will never allow us to enjoy the peace that comes through forgiveness until we have cast ourselves on His mercy, realizing that it is His law we have violated and that only He can offer forgiveness to the offender. Such forgiveness comes through the cross of Jesus where our debts to God were paid and where guilt is once-and-for-all removed.

Once again, what God requires, He provides to those who will humble themselves and look to Him for the answers to life's ultimate questions. What past failures are eating at you to the degree that any chance for future success is stifled? Give it to God, embrace His provision, and feel what its like, perhaps for the first time, to be free.

Chapter Ten

The God Conclusion!

That evening with Laura and her staff will remain one of the most dramatic events of my life. In the midst of everything, I thought of Michelangelo's painting where God, with a contorted face and an outstretched arm, is reaching down to man, while man, in contrasting apathy, nonchalantly lifts his hand toward God.

Indeed, man's greatest efforts are spent not in attempting to answer the most penetrating questions of our universe. Rather, if you travel to most universities in America, you will enter classrooms in which the discussions focus on attempting to debunk God. As I said earlier, for someone whom the educators of this land say does not exist, He sure gets a lot of attention.

The reality is that many do not want a world where God exists. With God comes responsibility. And we are so addicted to our supposed freedom that we are blinded to the fact that God's law is designed to protect and free, not bind. But this generation simply does not want to be told what to do by anyone, including God, even if it's for our own strength and well-being.

Proclaiming that God's law is not given arbitrarily is irrelevant to this crowd. Even if God's motivation is to protect, we don't care. *We want to be the judge of what is good for us.* So, the story of Genesis 1–3 continues to be played out every day in much of the world. We still refuse to live within God's boundaries. Accordingly, we keep going our own way, convinced that our way is the best way even though we are leaving a trail of carnage behind. Still, we never stop to think that perhaps we are the cause of all of this. Instead, we point toward heaven and scream, "God, where are you? Why did you let this happen?"

While it may be true that the world in which we live is deplorable in many ways, we simply must realize two things.

First, as we have stated above, most of what is happening in our world is the result of free-will creatures bent on self-aggrandizement, self-centeredness, and a "look out for number one" attitude. If we are so concerned about the pain and suffering in this world, what are we doing to change it? Blaming God is the easy way out. What activity in your life reveals your displeasure with the deplorable situation in which many people live? Are you a servant? Do you sacrifice your *wants* to meet other people's *needs*?

While most of us are praying, "God, why don't you do something about all the pain and suffering in this world," God is saying, "Is there no one down there who is willing to give up their own convenience and luxuries for a greater cause than themselves?"

Although many Americans do not want to hear this, contentment can coexist with sacrifice. Unfortunately, sacrifice is not a popular practice in our culture! The flesh is strong and begs continually to be fed. Even though feeding discontentment breeds even more discontentment, we continue to engage in such activity.

The God Conclusion!

Consider the impact of a life lived with a "wartime mentality" as expressed by John Piper in his book, *Don't Waste Your Life.*

The entire nation . . . seemed overnight to have snapped out of its Depression-era lethargy. Everyone scrambled to be of help. Rubber was needed for the war effort, and gasoline, and metal. A women's basketball game at Northwestern University was stopped so that the referee and all ten players could scour the floor for the lost bobby pin. Americans pitched in to support strict rationing programs and their boys turned out as volunteers in various collection drives. Soon butter and milk were restricted along with canned goods and meat. Shoes became scarce, and paper, and silk. People grew "victory gardens" and drove at the gas-saving "victory speed" of thirty-five miles an hour. "Use it up, wear it out, make it do, or do without?" became a popular slogan. Air-raid sirens and blackouts were scrupulously obeyed. America sacrificed.[32]

What is the point of all of this? So many are willing to point the finger at God, accusing Him of sitting on His hands while the world experiences so much pain and suffering, yet few are willing to do anything about it themselves. Why? Because sacrificing for a cause greater than ourselves is extremely unpopular in a country that is consumed with consumption and convenience.

My generation is so addicted to living for our own pleasures that it is difficult for us to fathom a life that gives up anything. We often accuse God because it is easy to do so. We do not want to take the time to do anything to help the rest of the world, so we say, "Let's take the easy way out; let's blame God!" Instead of blaming God, perhaps we should say, "Here am I; send me."

Father Joseph Damien is a poignant example of a life sent by God to alleviate suffering. He left his home in Belgium to assist leprosy patients in the middle of the South Pacific. He quickly grew to love these people, though his love expressed to them eventually took its toll.

One morning, as Father Damien was preparing the coffee and tea, he accidentally spilled some scalding hot water on his foot. To his utter shock and horror, he realized he could feel no pain! He had become like those with whom he had shared his life.[33]

Yes, there is much pain and injustice in the world, but God is actively combating it through the lives of people who have turned to Him and committed their lives to a purpose greater than themselves.

Second, while there may be much that is undesirable about this world, there is still so much good, and it is true that the best things in life are free.

After my mom died, I would often go into times of depression. When I found it difficult to snap out of it, I would drive forty minutes west of Auckland to Muriwai Beach. The Kiwis really know how to keep beautiful sites free from commercial ruin. Muriwai beach is a prime example where the coastline remains unspoiled. Just over the hill from Muriwai Beach you will find two gigantic rocks that rise out of the middle of the ocean. These rocks serve as the home to a gannet colony.

These birds, which migrate from Australia, are magnificent! The beauty of the Tasman Sea coupled with the constant flight of these birds scouring for food makes this spot on Auckland's North Shore one of the most peaceful places on earth.

Upon arrival I would find a spot out of the wind where I could take in the beauty of God's creation. If I got hungry, I would mosey on down to the fish and chips shop for a bit of sustenance. For the most part, however, I was content to simply lean back and take it all in. I am thankful for Muriwai Beach and the emotional healing I often found there.

The older I get, the more I long for places like Muriwai Beach. Just a few weeks ago I traveled back to Zimbabwe, returning once again to Victoria Falls. Viewing the falls is absolutely breathtaking! Words will never do it justice! You just gotta go! Each night, just before sunset, we sat out on the deck of our hotel (The Victoria Falls Safari Lodge) and watched the elephants, impalas, baboons, warthogs, waterbuck, and other wildlife come to the watering hole for a late evening drink. We all agreed we wished those evenings would never end.

Of course there are so many other grand things about this world. Families, friends, lattés, chocolate, and more. The unfortunate circumstances to which we are all susceptible are a present reality. Even so, most of us would live again if we had the chance. Although there is so much evil in this world, God still preserves so much good in order that He may continually draw us into relationship. He draws us not only because He loves us and wants the best for us but also that He may use us for His purposes—to combat the effects of free-will decisions that wreak havoc on those whom He loves.

Sadly, and this is what this book is really about, the issues that keep us from God have not been thoroughly thought through, and the arguments we make against God are not only illogical but, in most cases, self-defeating.

God is not going to wipe out evil by removing free will. For the present time He is going to protect the integrity of love because it is the highest value in His universe. And if love is so important to God, imagine the measure of affection and care one receives when he/she submits to the will of God and enters into this loving relationship. Where there is God, every good thing exists.

In the meantime, while you and I live in this world, we should live our lives for God's purposes. In doing so we discover that everything for which we are searching in this life is found. Not only do we recover God, we recover ourselves, our purpose, our destiny. I had such a life-changing experience during the summer of 2007 when I was given the opportunity to visit the prisons of Rwanda. As we stepped off the plane in Kigali, we could sense the fear and oppression left over from the 1994 genocide. During a period of 90 days, over 800,000 Tutsis were massacred at the hands of machete-wielding Hutus. Tribal warfare in Africa is as old as the continent itself. What is new to this century however is the growing popularity of reconciliation commissions designed to promote forgiveness rather than retaliation. Following Nelson Mandela's lead in South Africa, the Rwandan government offers freedom to the Hutus guilty of participating in the genocide in exchange for their confessions. Such confessions must be publicly stated and directly addressed to the families which have been offended by the Hutu prisoner. Our purpose was to go into these Rwandan prisons and encourage the Hutus to confess their crimes to both God and man and seek forgiveness.

Not until we were driving through the streets of Kigali did I realize the magnitude and danger of what we were about to do. Having lived in Zimbabwe for six years I had grown accustomed to the smiling, playful faces of the Shona people. In Kigali however, no such smiles existed. The stench of death, anger, and revenge, although not as strong as years gone by, still lingered. As we checked into the hotel (not Hotel Rwanda by any stretch of the imagination), the thought of what we were actually getting ready to do sank in. I began to think of my wife and children and perhaps not getting back to them in one piece! As we made our way out of the city into the countryside toward the prison, my apprehension increased.

Arriving at the prison and noticing that the warden resided "outside" the prison walls did not help matters much. A tall, powerful-looking man of few words basically said that we had 35 minutes to get in and get out. When they opened the gates to the prison, the reality hit. Eleven thousand detainees living in a prison designed for 4000 inmates made our task extremely difficult. As we walked through a sea of people toward the platform from which we would address the crowd, the stares seemed hollow and empty. What took probably three minutes seemed like an eternity as we thought about the fact that we were now within closed walls face to face with thousands of men and women whose lives hung in the balance.

After the men with whom I traveled decided I would be the one to address the crowd, I grabbed my Bible, turned to the prisoners and began to speak. I am not sure which was the most astounding: the fact that what I had spent so much time preparing no longer seemed appropriate or that the voice of God seemed to be saying to me, "Jeff, just be willing, and I will give you the words to speak." No sooner did this thought depart than the next one appeared. Bolting into my mind was a children's story that I had read a few years ago. Imagine. A children's story to machete murderers! What was I thinking? Nevertheless, I was confident that this was where God wanted me to go, and so, I went.

It's a story about a little boy and little girl (brother and sister) who each gathered a jar of treasures. One collected candy, the other marbles. One day, the little boy asked his sister to consider trading all her candy for all his marbles. She agreed. However, the night before the trade was to occur, the little boy dipped his hand into his jar and removed five of the most precious stones. The night after the exchange the little sister slept soundly but the little boy could not sleep at all. Wandering the halls he kept thinking to himself, "I wonder if my sister gave me all her candy."

Upon hearing what the little boy had done to his sister, the crowd booed. I found this shocking. After all, these were machete murderers! How bad can stealing a few marbles really be? At any rate, at the conclusion of the story, the reason for God's use of a simple story became clear as I knelt down to the ground, looked up toward the heavens and exclaimed, "If you will give God all your sin, He will give you all His forgiveness"

At that moment hands began to move toward the air as a wave of repentance swept through the prison and my interpreter began to seize the moment to further prick the hearts of these prisoners. As our time expired and we made our way through the crowd toward the iron gates, hollow stares became smiles of appreciation as the arms and hands of the prisoners reached out in gratitude for the message we had brought. When they closed the iron gates behind us, I realized at that moment that I had never before felt so alive. Filled with the meaning and purpose that accompanies self-sacrifice, I began to understand what it really means to live.

This I believe is the key to finding what seems to elude so many. Self-preservation is not the key to living life to the full. Self-sacrifice and living our life for a purpose greater than ourselves is the key to discovering the abundant life. This self-sacrifice is directly related to our belief or disbelief in God. With God, a purpose greater than ourselves exists. Without Him, no other meaning, purpose, or significance can survive. Moreover, life becomes a journey of self-preservation that always ends in the same way . . . death.

End Notes

Introduction

[1] This is a typical practice of the African crocodile.

[2] Frederick Hoyle, *The Intelligent Universe* (New York: Holt, Rinehart, and Winston, 1983) 19.

Chapter One

[3] David Hume, source unknown.

[4] This line of reasoning is not at all original with me. I have been heavily influenced by Dr. Ravi Zacharias. In fact, I have studied his response to the skeptic so often that I have been able to memorize Dr. Zacharias's opening lines. These are the words I often use to answer the question of evil. Likewise, Dr. Zacharias also sparked my interest in the Nuremburg Trials and in the Holocaust as it relates to evil in this world.

[5] Ravi Zacharias, *Cries of the Heart* (Nashville: Word, 1998) 108-109.

[6] Ibid, 109.

Chapter Two

[7] Ravi Zacharias, *Is Your Church Ready?* (Grand Rapids: Zondervan, 2003) back cover paraphrase.

[8] Bill Hybels, *Fanning the Flames of Marriage: Help for Husbands*. Audio-cassette. Willow Creek Association, M869.

[9] Lyrics by Boudleaux Bryant and performed by Nazareth, *Nazareth's Greatest Hits*, 1975.

[10] G.K. Chesterton as quoted in *Cries of the Heart*, 173.

[11] I heard Wayne Cordeiro, Pastor of New Hope Christian Center in Oahu, Hawaii, use this illustration during a message in 1998 delivered at Farrington High School.

Chapter Three

[12] C.S. Lewis, *The Problem of Pain* (New York: Macmillan, 1966) 138.

[13] Deepak Chopra, *The Seven Spiritual Laws of Success* (San Rafael, CA: Amber Allen, 1994) 68, 69.

[14] "God-botherers" is a term most New Zealanders use to describe any person who, when discussing any social issue, introduces the word, "God."

[15] Garth George, "Why Did God Allow This to Happen?" *Auckland Herald*, January 6, 2005.

End Notes

[16] See Ravi Zacharias, *Cries of the Heart*, 78-80.

[17] When we speak of God taking risks, we do not mean to imply that God was unaware that many would use their freedom to reject Him. God, like us, thinks in logical progression. The entire creation scenario would have been thought through before the first man was created. Although God foresaw the rebellion of many men and women, He also foresaw the love of many who would desire relationship with Him. Seeing this love relationship, God decided to move forward with His plan to create, while at the same time working in and through history to reconcile man back to Himself.

Chapter Four

[18] Corrie ten Boom, *The Hiding Place* (Alresford, Hants: Christian Literature Crusade, 1971) 13 of bonus section.

[19] David Wallington, *The Secret Room: The Story of Corrie ten Boom* (13 April 2006): Online. http://www.gloryofhiscross.org/corrie.htm.

Chapter Five

[20] As told by Ravi Zacharias, *Jesus among Other Gods*, Compact disc. Ravi Zacharias International Ministries, Norcross, GA. CD 137.

[21] He is one of the finest Luthiers in the United States. His guitars are masterfully crafted and his website (vinesguitars.com) receives much attention.

Chapter Six

[22] We need to be careful of assuming that children who grow up in the third world are miserable. Never have I seen such joy and laughter as when I attended a soccer game in the bush of Zimbabwe in a little village called Chidamoyo. The children who attended the tiny mission school had nothing more than life's basics, but enthusiastically exuded gladness and joy.

[23] Lee Strobel, "What Would You Ask God? Why Is There Suffering?" Sermon Transcript M9928, Willow Creek Community Church (Chicago: 1999) 6.

[24] Warren W. Wiersbe, *Classic Sermons on Suffering* (Grand Rapids: Kregel, 1984) 92.

[25] Lee Strobel quoting Peter Kreeft in *The Case for Faith*, 67.

Chapter Seven

[26] Although not enforced, adultery is still illegal in America.

Chapter Eight

[27] C.S. Lewis, *The Problem of Pain*, 129-130.

Chapter Nine

[28] Eusebius's words are quoted by Dr. Alexander Metherell in Lee Strobel's *The Case for Faith*, 261.

[29] Seneca, Dialogue 3:2.2.

[30] Lee Strobel, *The Case for Faith*, 262-267.

[31] Many will read this section and accuse Christians of creating a need and then claiming to have that which will satisfy it. The need to deal with the guilt associated with violating a moral law, however, is a universal reality present within every culture and society whether Christian or not. One must take notice that only the Christian faith offers a sin-bearer who has provided a way in which guilt can be removed once and for all. All other religions grant a temporary solution to guilt that lasts only until the next violation. Jesus, by way of the cross, offers a one-time solution to past, present, and future guilt. When we embrace His sacrifice for our sin, we no longer stand in condemnation (Romans 8:1). We may experience conviction by God's spirit to change directions and do that which is good so that we may enjoy the abundant life, but this is different from guilt. Guilt occurs when we have broken the law of God and are required to pay the penalty. Since Jesus paid the penalty for all who submit their lives to Him and live for a purpose greater than themselves, guilt is eternally removed. Conviction still comes however as a means to spur us on toward the life we have always wanted.

Chapter Ten

[32] John Piper, *Don't Waste Your Life* (Wheaton, IL: Crossway Books, 2003) 116.

[33] When Joseph Damien died, Belgium declared him a national hero and demanded that his body be flown back to Belgium, but the people of Molokai protested. To the lepers, he was their hero! He should not leave the people to whom he showed such great compassion. He did not leave them in life, neither should he leave them in death.

After much bargaining, red tape, and bureaucracy, the country of Belgium and the Island of Molokai finally reached an agreement. The people of this tiny island in the South Pacific proclaimed to the Belgian government, "You can have Father Damien's body. Only allow us to cut off his right arm and bury it here on the island because this is the arm that extended so much mercy, love, and compassion to us." Belgium agreed.

"What the Bible Says" Book Club Series

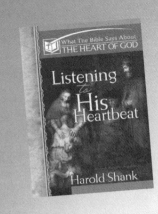

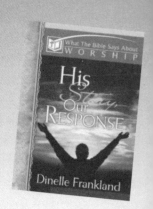

WTBS Suffering

Where is God When We Suffer? addresses the topic from various perspectives. It begins with Lynn's own personal story of loss and suffering. Dr. Gardner then guides us through a study of both Old and New Testament examples of people who suffer. Why did they? How did they deal with it? What can we learn from their experiences? This book also includes a philosophical discussion of evil and suffering for those who want an analysis of this difficult topic from a biblical perspective. How can an all-powerful, all-loving God permit such pain and tragedy in the world He created?

Welcome to The Club...

What does the Bible say about that? Have you ever been asked this question or wondered for yourself? If the Bible is the ultimate authority on life and relationships, then it is the essential source of guidance to impact our everyday decisions. The "What the Bible Says" series will take an exhaustive look at each subject matter.

When you enroll in our "What the Bible Says" book club, you will receive a 30% discount on each title. A new title will be sent to you automatically upon each release (3-4 per year).

To enroll, please call 1-800-289-3300; or email your name, address, phone number to books@collegepress.com.